Associate Staff Ministry

Associate
Staff Ministry

Thriving Personally, Professionally, and Relationally

Kevin E. Lawson and **Mick Boersma**

An Alban Institute Book

ROWMAN & LITTLEFIELD
Lanham • Boulder • New York • London

Published by Rowman & Littlefield
A wholly owned subsidiary of The Rowman & Littlefield Publishing Group, Inc.
4501 Forbes Boulevard, Suite 200, Lanham, Maryland 20706
www.rowman.com

16 Carlisle Street, London W1D 3BT, United Kingdom

British Library Cataloguing in Publication Information Available

Library of Congress Cataloging-in-Publication Data

Lawson, Kevin E. (Kevin Ethan), 1956–
   Associate staff ministry : thriving personally, professionally, and relationally /
Kevin E. Lawson and Mick Boersma.
      pages cm
   Revised and expanded from author's How to thrive in associate staff ministry,
c2000.
   Includes bibliographical references.
   ISBN 978-1-56699-761-4 (cloth : alk. paper)–ISBN 978-1-56699-442-2 (pbk. : alk.
paper)–ISBN 978-1-56699-752-2 (electronic) 1. Group ministry. 2. Church
officers. I. Title.
   BV675 .L38 2014
   253–dc23   2013020755

♾™ The paper used in this publication meets the minimum requirements of
American National Standard for Information Sciences–Permanence of Paper for
Printed Library Materials, ANSI/NISO Z39.48-1992.

Printed in the United States of America

Contents

Foreword

Much has changed since the original *How to Thrive in Associate Staff Ministry* by Kevin E. Lawson was published over a decade ago. As a proportion of church budgets, staff beyond the lead pastor has grown more than any other category. There are a number of reasons for this change. While the growth of large churches is one factor, staff positions are now found in churches of all sizes. Whether in large or mid-size churches, many of these positions are part-time. More associate staff are coming out of the congregations where they serve rather than being recruited from elsewhere. While those serving as associate pastors tend to have theological education comparable to lead pastors, many other professional associate staff are trained in fields often useful to their ministry but may or may not have formal theological education. Some associate staff are ordained, but many are not. Many seminary graduates come from larger, suburban churches where associate staff positions are a given. For them, such ministry has always been an option, especially since many were shaped by such staff.

All these changes make the revised and expanded edition of *Associate Staff Ministry: Thriving Personally, Professionally, and Relationally* by Lawson and Mick Boersma even more important. For many years there was a gap in congregational leadership literature on the role of associate pastors and other professional staff members. Much of the writing on multiple staff ministry has been from the perspective of the senior pastor. Kevin Lawson made a major contribution in addressing the distinctive needs, circumstances, and opportunities of staff ministry in his original book. This expanded study draws from a larger base of associate staff and rich insights from the authors.

In *Associate Staff Ministry*, the authors combine in a masterful way scholarly research skills with their experience in multiple congregations of different denominations. The research methods are solid, and the illustrations from their experience of local church staff studied will ring true to those in associate staff ministry.

There is a renewed appreciation today in the church for the importance of "practices" in one's growth in Christian discipleship. Likewise, in the business world there is much emphasis on the study of "best practices" within particular industries as a way to learn from the example of others in order to improve. In essence, the authors are drawing from both of these important understandings in their approach to studying staff ministry.

There are challenges associated with staff ministry, but the dominant theme of the book is ministry enhancement, not problem solving. They identify long-serving staff ministers who are thriving in such ministry. They name those practices that promote longevity, satisfaction, and personal well-being. The corollary goal is to find ways that staff ministers, as well as their supervising pastors and lay committees, can incorporate these practices to support the vitality of congregational ministry and mission. Their model of concentric circles that include thriving personally, thriving relationally, and thriving professionally—all supported by church leadership—can be important for staff and church leaders. All have responsibilities and opportunities to which they need to hold one another accountable.

The positive and constructive stance of this book makes it a valuable resource. Often enormous energy is misspent around matters of standing and prerogative, since staff members normally suffer from lower status, salary, influence, and job security. Lawson and Boersma correctly frame the issues around one's calling to ministry.

In Luke 22:24 a dispute arises among the disciples as to "which one of them was to be regarded as the greatest." This is the wrong question, but one that is asked all too often within church staffs. Authority in the Bible has to do with a responsibility, not a privilege. Christian authority is not about our status in relationship to others but what God's will is for each of us and how faithful we are in fulfilling God's call.

Letty Russell speaks of the "power of purpose" in contrast to the "power of position." It is the church's mission and the vision for a particular congregation that must guide all ministries among the ordained, staff, and laity. Christian authority is always about the fulfillment of

God's vision. When leaders take their eyes off the larger vision and focus instead on where they stand in relationship to others in a hierarchy, then energy is misdirected and leadership ceases to be faithful.

Instead of asking, "Who is to be regarded as greatest among us?" leaders and congregations might more productively ask these questions:

- What is your particular calling from God? (Calling)
- Do you have what you need to fulfill your calling? (Support)
- Are you being faithful in fulfilling your calling? (Accountability)

These questions put the focus not on one's status in relationship to others but instead on one's relationship to God's vision for oneself.

In the marvelous wisdom of God, all of God's servants may then come to experience power not as a fixed sum that must be appropriated all so carefully. Instead, power will become an infinitely expandable sum as all become strong for their particular callings and, at the same time, make sure that all other colleagues are strong for their own callings. We also come to see that all of us have authority in different ways based on the unique callings that God, the church, and our context place upon us.

Lovett H. Weems Jr.
Distinguished Professor of Church Leadership
Director, Lewis Center for Church Leadership
Wesley Theological Seminary
Washington, DC

Acknowledgments

With a deep sense of satisfaction and gratitude we offer this revised and expanded book to those who serve as associate staff members. Our lives have been bound up in ministry leadership and in preparing, equipping, and supporting others entering into ministry, most often in associate staff roles. Our sense of satisfaction has grown as we have worked together on this effort, learning from each other and from the many associate staff members we have interacted with in focus groups and through our surveys. We feel that with all the help we have received, we have something significant to offer to those who take on ministry leadership roles in the church and to those who support and supervise them.

We also have a deep sense of gratitude, because this project grows out of the support provided by several groups in two major research efforts. In 1996–97, The Louisville Institute provided major funding for the "Thriving in Associate Staff Ministry" research project that Kevin undertook. In addition, the North American Professors of Christian Education (NAPCE) and Biola University contributed grants to make that first round of research possible. Many professional organizations cooperated in the focus-group phase of that study, including the Professional Association of Christian Educators (PACE), Youth Specialties, the International Network of Children's Pastors (INCP), MusiCalifornia, Hume Lake Conference Center, the Dallas (Texas) Southern Baptist Church Association, and many friends in ministry in Canada and Southern California. In addition, Kevin received help from leaders in many denominational offices who provided assistance with the survey portion of the study. In 2012, as we (Mick and Kevin) undertook the second study, we received assistance from our school, Talbot School of Theology, Biola University. The alumni office covered the costs of our focus groups, and Kevin benefited from a partial research leave to devote attention to the revision of this book.

In the 1996–97 study, many people assisted with data analysis, making Kevin's task easier. Special thanks to Christy Morr and Doris Anderson, who typed transcripts of the focus-group sessions; Dave Keehn and Brent Hinsley, who helped lead and analyze the youth-pastor focus groups; Shelly Cunningham, who helped lead some focus groups of women associate staff members; and students at Canadian Theological Seminary, who helped him process much of the focus-group data in a course he taught as guest faculty.

In the study just completed (2012), we benefited from the help of another two hundred veteran associate staff members who responded to our survey, and another twenty in Southern California who joined us over lunches for focus-group discussions of what we had learned from our surveys. In addition, Tanya Wheeldon, who serves as administrative assistant to Kevin, helped us prepare for our focus groups, and our spouses provided encouragement and support to us in both our research and our writing. Thanks to all of you for helping make this research and this book possible.

May this book assist and encourage those who want to serve, and those who now serve in associate staff positions in church and para-church settings.

Introduction to the Second Edition
A Model for Thriving in Associate Staff Ministry

What does it take to thrive, not just survive, as an associate staff member in the local church, and how can a person get to that point?

Too many people who begin serving in associate staff ministry find it to be a draining experience and don't stay with it long. While it is true that some are using associate work as an opportunity to gain experience and skills to move into a senior or solo pastoral role, many others have no such vocational goals. Associate staff ministry positions are where they intend to stay, but over time they encounter significant problems that cause them to leave in frustration. Still others stay but hang on in a survival mode with little joy or satisfaction in their ministry. How did this state of affairs come to be, and what can be done to improve it?

This book, both the original edition and this revised and expanded edition, was written to help church workers break out of a survival mode in ministry and reach the point of thriving as associate staff members. But what does it mean to thrive in associate staff ministry and not merely survive? Because the boundary between these two experiences can be a little fuzzy, it may be helpful to begin by looking at each experience in its extreme.

We each probably have our own intuitive sense of what it means to thrive in our work. If we had to describe it, we might speak of having a sense of personal well-being, contentment, and satisfaction in our ministry. We might even talk about finding joy and fulfillment in our work. Our involvement in this ministry, though difficult at times, is energizing, not draining. This sense of thriving is not necessarily due to the ministry going smoothly, because that state of affairs can fluctuate. The ability to thrive is based not on the absence of stress or frustrating situations but on the ability to continue to work in the midst of them, not growing excessively discouraged or drained by them.

In contrast, if we had to describe the experience of barely surviving, we might complain of feeling drained by work responsibilities and feeling that life is stressful and out of balance. Dissatisfaction and a lack of contentment mark how we view our ministry. We gain little sense of fulfillment from our ministry, even when things are going smoothly. The work might get done, and we might cope with the stresses, but our work is only a matter of survival and going through the motions.

What we share in this book is based on two research efforts—one in 1996–97, the other in 2012—that explored the experiences of long-term associate staff members who felt that they were thriving in their ministry leadership roles. (See appendix A for a description of these two studies.) In the responses of more than four hundred long-term associate staff members in fourteen denominations in the United States and Canada to the 1997 survey, and in the almost two hundred responses to the 2012 survey, the extremes of really thriving and barely surviving were described this way:

> A person who is really thriving: *This is a good ministry fit. I enjoy what I am doing. I find my work to be very satisfying. In the midst of ministry demands, I am finding ways to sustain my personal well-being. I am not eager to consider some alternative kind of work or ministry.*

> A person who is barely surviving: *This ministry is very frustrating. I do not enjoy what I am doing. I find little satisfaction in my work. In the midst of my ministry demands, I find that I am drained. I am doing what I need to, but I would gladly consider some alternative kind of work or ministry.*

While we all may have days when we feel that we're just surviving, a ministry consistently characterized by this feeling is a difficult one in which to continue—difficult but not impossible. God can be a tremendous source of encouragement and strength in seasons of distress, enabling us to persevere in fulfilling difficult ministry responsibilities. As prophets such as Jeremiah found, faithfulness in following God's will does not always guarantee a sense of thriving, though it can bring contentment if we are open to it.

As nice as a sense of thriving can be, personal satisfaction and well-being are not our primary goals in ministry; serving God is. However, following God through serving the church in associate staff ministry positions can be a growing and rewarding experience, a source of fulfillment and joy, and not just a matter of survival. The good news is that many people who serve in associate staff positions report that they are thriving. Between the 1997 survey and the 2012 survey, approximately six hundred long-term staff members have described what has contributed to their sense of thriving and what others might do to experience it as well.

Background on Associate Staff Ministry

In North America, the number of congregations with associate staff members and congregations with more than one associate staff member is growing. Some denominations list in their national directories almost as many associate staff as senior or solo pastors. These associate staff people serve their churches in a variety of ways. Some focus their ministry efforts on children, youth, adults, families, or general educational ministries. Others serve in the areas of worship and music. Some are involved in pastoral care and counseling, and others focus on administration. Still others carry more than one kind of responsibility. Not all these staff members are ordained. Many are in the process of seeking ordination, but others are "licensed" staff members. Their denominations recognize their gifts and calling to ministry, but for various reasons they do not have full ordained status. In some cases, this is an issue of academic preparation, scope of ministry responsibilities, or gender. Still other staff members are neither ordained nor licensed but are laypeople who have entered ministerial work as a vocation.

Historically, associate staff positions can be traced to apprenticeship arrangements in which the minister in training learned the ministry by assisting an experienced pastor of a congregation in his or her duties. This type of associate staff arrangement was temporary and intermittent. With the exception of some music staff positions (for example, organist, choir director), the development of permanent associate staff positions is primarily a twentieth- to twenty-first-century phenomenon. It had its beginnings in the late nineteenth century with the growth of church religious education efforts and in the early twentieth century with the development of degree programs to prepare people to become directors of religious education (DREs). These DREs oversaw the educational ministries of a congregation in much the same way a principal gives leadership to a school.

As local churches grew and became sensitive to a variety of focused ministry needs, the demand for associate staff members, both generalists and specialists, increased. However, the growth of this ministry field has been accompanied by a variety of stresses and problems. In general, associate staff positions have been characterized by relatively brief tenures and high attrition rates. For associate staff in educational ministry areas, Paul H. Veith, a Christian education professor writing in the 1940s, summarized the problems in these words:

> Whereas the missionary has status and security, the professionally trained worker in Christian education has neither. He has only confused standards, inadequate recognition, poor salary, almost no job security, little help in placement if it becomes necessary for him to make a change; and there is a tendency to regard him as superannuated by the time he reaches middle life.[1]

Even today, in comparison with solo or senior pastors, associate staff members tend to have lower status in the congregation, lower salaries, and little job security. The work of many tends to be less visible to congregation members, resulting in fewer expressions of appreciation or support. Some denominations have a policy that when the senior pastor of a church resigns, associate staff members must offer their resignations to the new senior pastor. This practice increases the uncertainty surrounding associate staff positions. The situation varies to some degree from one denomination to another, but many factors work against thriving long term as an associate staff member.

The good news, however, is that many people do thrive in associate staff ministry positions. Across North America thousands of church workers are flourishing in associate staff ministries. They have moved past the survival mode and find real satisfaction and joy in ministry. The results of our studies revealed and reinforced that the ability to thrive in associate staff ministry tends to be influenced by four major dimensions of our lives. This book is structured around those four important areas, and we use a diagram of concentric rings to illustrate their relationship to one another. The diagram will be explained in more detail in each of the four sections of the book.

A Model for Thriving in Associate Staff Ministry

Elements of Thriving in Associate Staff Ministry

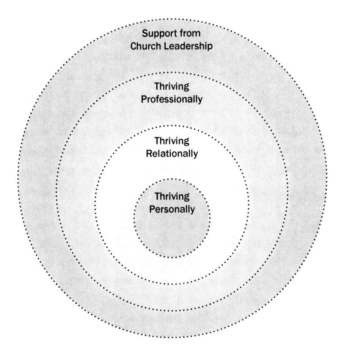

First (Inner) Circle = Thriving Personally—Part 1
We must have inner spiritual and emotional strength through our relationship with God in order to thrive.

Second Circle = Thriving Relationally—Part 2
Ministry is done through building into and benefitting from supportive relationships.

Third Circle = Thriving Professionally—Part 3
Developing and maintaining supportive working conditions and increasing ministry competencies is critical for thriving.

Fourth (Outer) Circle = Support from Church Leadership—Part 4
Supervisors and boards show support by creating an environment conducive to thriving in associate ministry.

Part 1: Thriving Personally

In Proverbs 4:23 we read, "Keep your heart with all vigilance, for from it flow the springs of life." Foundational to associate staff members' ability to thrive in ministry is the vitality of our relationship with God, our ability to discern and follow God's call on our lives and to both savor the joys of ministry and weather the stresses that inevitably come as we serve.

Part 2: Thriving Relationally

Paul writes to the Romans, "So we, though many, are one body in Christ, and individually members one of another" (12:5). Because associate staff are part of the one body of Christ, ministry involves relationships, and God uses a variety of relationships to strengthen and stretch us as we serve. Healthy family relationships, work relationships, and supportive relationships with others outside our families and work settings all contribute to our ability to thrive in ministry.

Part 3: Thriving Professionally

In his letter to the Colossians, Paul writes, "Whatever you do, work heartily, as for the Lord and not for men, knowing that from the Lord you will receive the inheritance as your reward. You are serving the Lord Christ" (3:23–24). How we as associate staff members approach our work makes a difference in how we experience it. Both the circumstances of our work settings and our own internal attitudes and commitments that shape how we respond to these circumstances are important influences on our thriving as we serve.

Part 4: Support from Church Leadership

In Paul's first letter to Timothy, he states, "Let the elders who rule well be considered worthy of double honor, especially those who labor in preaching and teaching" (5:17). How can those who have responsibility for the supervision and support of associate staff members best "honor" them? Both ministry supervisors and church boards have important roles to play in helping associate staff members thrive in their ministries. This section is intended to be shared with those in these important roles.

Mick and I (Kevin) invite you to read and consider what we have learned from the hundreds of veteran, thriving associate staff who participated in our two studies. There is much wisdom in what they have to share, and we can all learn from their experiences. We pray that this book will be used by God to help you increase in your own sense of thriving in the ministry role you are in or as you seek a position in which to serve.

Part 1

Thriving Personally

Introduction

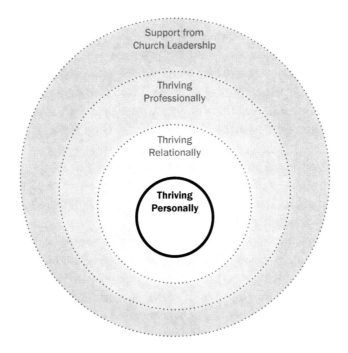

Support from
Church Leadership

Thriving
Professionally

Thriving
Relationally

**Thriving
Personally**

Foundational to any sense of thriving in life is our own sense of purpose and well-being. Both of these are rooted in our relationship with the triune God who has created us, has entered into relationship with us through Jesus Christ, and guides us through the ongoing work of the Holy Spirit. Our work is only one aspect of our lives in general. For most of us, though, our work experiences are a major part of our overall sense of thriving. If we struggle with our understanding of what we ought to be doing vocationally, we may struggle to maintain a sense of satisfaction with the direction of our lives. In addition, if we feel distant from God, we can struggle more with our sense of purpose and in coping with the emotional challenges of our work experiences.

This first section of the book focuses on the personal aspects of thriving in ministry. One of the strongest themes that emerged from the focus groups and surveys that we conducted with approximately six hundred long-term associate staff members has to do with their sense of calling to serve in vocational ministry. This is the focus of chapter 1. In it we examine the types of calling one experiences in life, how God brings about those senses of calling, and why this is so important to one's thriving in associate staff ministry. The chapter includes questions to help you consider your own sense of calling and how to renew it if it is flagging.

Another strong theme from the research we carried out had to do with the importance of maintaining one's spiritual vitality in the demands of ministry. In chapter 2 we look at a number of foundational spiritual practices that long-term associate staff say are critical to maintaining their own spiritual health as they serve the needs of others. A number of creative ideas are shared to help you find ways to pursue your own spiritual growth in the midst of a busy schedule. Spiritual dryness is not an uncommon experience for those in ministry, and we also discuss ways to move through the dry spells and back into a renewed walk with God.

People who thrive in associate staff ministry report that their work brings with it many stresses and times of discouragement and struggle. In spite of those struggles, they have found ways to draw maximum encouragement from the joys of ministry and ways of coping with the stresses that inevitably come. In chapter 3 we look at the range of joys that come with associate staff ministry and how to savor them. We also consider the many sources of stress in ministry and a range of ways to cope with the stresses we experience. It is not always easy, but God does give us ways to navigate these struggles and maintain personal well-being.

So, this book starts with a close look at ourselves, our calling, our ongoing relationship with God, and how we respond to the ups and downs of ministry that we all experience. Listen to what our sisters and brothers in ministry have to share, and reflect on your own calling, spiritual vitality, and ability to savor the joys and cope with the stresses of ministry. This is a critical place to begin.

1

Finding Satisfaction in Following God's Call

Ministry is not an occupation but a vocation. It primarily depends not on professional credentials but the ability to hear and heed the call of God.[1] —BEN PATTERSON

"When are you going to get your own church?" That was a question I (Kevin) heard several times during the years I served as a minister of education in congregations in Nebraska, New Jersey, and Maine. The expectation was that if I was called to "the ministry," then someday I would be the pastor of my own church. Often, my response to these questions was, "I have my own church; it is right here." I had a sense that this was where I belonged, serving in the ways I was serving, and I was content to do so. Some people had difficulty thinking that I could be satisfied serving as an associate staff member. Others just assumed that a calling to vocational ministry (the vocation of ministerial leadership) would naturally lead to a move to the senior pastoral role.

What is *calling*, anyway? How does it relate to thriving in ministry? Does one have to be *called* to serve in a ministerial role? What does *calling* look like? How does it happen? What difference does it make in the midst of ministry demands? In this chapter we will look at these issues, but let me begin first with a story about my own experience of calling and the ups and downs of vocational ministry as an associate staff member.

As a high-school student I had plans to pursue studies in forestry engineering and to spend my life working in and enjoying the wilderness. When I came to faith in Christ, God gave me a new desire to work with people and to help them grow in their walk with God. I did not have a sense of calling to be a pastor or to work in the church, but I did know that God wanted me to work with people, not trees.

As I pursued my undergraduate and graduate studies in Christian education, God called me to the church, to serve in developing and strengthening the educational ministries of congregations. This calling was not a dramatic event but a growing awareness and understanding through Scripture, prayer, and life experiences that this vocation was where I was to invest myself.

When I began my first associate staff position, I did so with the conviction that this place was where God wanted me and this work was what I was meant to do. In that first year the work was hard, but I saw signs of progress and received encouragement from many people. It was easy to feel that this was indeed my calling. By the second year, however, problems multiplied, and it was harder to see positive results from my work. My frustration grew, and I began to wonder if I was mistaken about God's direction. Shouldn't following God's call to ministry be easier than this? The senior pastor and I finally agreed that I should look for a new ministry position, but I was no longer sure what I should be doing. If God had called me to this work, then why was it so hard, and why wasn't it more successful? I explored other kinds of work, but I could not escape the conviction that God wanted me to serve in the church. I had no hope for satisfaction outside God's will, but I needed God's help if I was going to be effective and have any sense of thriving in ministry. It wasn't easy, but that help came over time as I strove to be faithful in following God's direction. I'll say more about my experience later in the chapter.

Calling: A Foundation for Thriving

God is the one who created us and knows us most intimately, including our personalities, character, abilities, desires, and needs (Ps. 139). Out of great love for us, God has brought us into restored fellowship, calling us to salvation through faith in Jesus Christ, our Lord and Savior. God has also given us gifts through the Holy Spirit (1 Cor. 12) and has created us for good works that have been prepared for us to do (Eph. 2:10). Therefore, our greatest satisfaction, joy, and fulfillment in life is to be found as we come to understand and follow God's will for our lives. Going our own way leads us away from God's will, that which can bring us true fulfillment in life.

For the sake of the church and the work of God's kingdom, God has instructed congregations to set apart individuals to devote themselves to leading and serving the fellowship and taking the gospel to the world. God has prepared these people and calls them to these tasks, to do these "good works." It is commonplace for pastors and missionaries to describe an experience or process by which God called them into vocational ministry. For some, it was a clear direction given at a specific time. For others, it was a gradual understanding that God wanted them to take on ministry responsibility. Whatever the process, many of these people describe how following God's call, though difficult at times, has been a source of satisfaction and fulfillment for them.

But what about associate staff members? Does God call them to ministry as well? Do they need a sense of calling from God to enable them to experience satisfaction and fulfillment in the face of their ministry demands? Do they need a calling to thrive in associate staff ministry? The answer is a resounding yes! The vast majority of the thriving associate staff members in our 1998 study (92 percent) said this was important in their ability to thrive in ministry. When we investigated this again in 2012, the figure had risen to 97 percent. Several explained how that calling had affected them in their ministry.

While involvement in ministry to others is a call that all Christians share (1 Cor. 12; Rom. 12; 1 Pet. 4:11–16), a few are appointed by God to serve the church vocationally in various servant-leader positions (Eph. 4:11). In *The Purpose of the Church and Its Ministry* (1956), theologian and sociologist of religion H. Richard Niebuhr, with Daniel Day Williams and James M. Gustafson, summarized four aspects of calling to vocational ministry, which provide a good framework for assessing one's own calling as an associate staff member.[2] I have adapted them below.

The Call to Be a Christian: Discipleship in the Body of Christ

The call to be a Christian is foundational to all other senses of calling. We are to first belong to Christ and follow him in obedience. Then, as part of the body of Christ, we are called to serve with the gifts we have been given. No one has to question whether one should be using his or her gifts and abilities in ministry to others. That is how God made the church to function, each person exercising the gifts that God has given as a means of grace to the body (1 Pet. 4:10). For a few this means ministry as a vocation, but it is a responsibility for everyone that comes with being "members one of another" (Eph. 4:25). In this sense, all are called. Those considering associate staff ministry need to consider the gifts and abilities God has given them and how these might be used in vocational ministry. Long-term associate staff who thrive in their ministries report that they have developed an awareness of their gifts, employing them in the types of ministry where they fit best.

The Secret Call: An Inner Sense of "Oughtness"

The second aspect of calling is the "secret call," an inner urgency to serve God as one's vocation.[3] Most thriving associate staff members report that they have a clear sense of calling from God to serve in an associate staff ministry. For some, this secret call is a general call to serve the church; for others, it is focused on a particular area of ministry, such as children's ministry or music and worship. One facet of this secret call mentioned by several veteran associate staff, one that has contributed to their flourishing in ministry, is an understanding that they are called to a support role, not to a senior pastorate. One associate pastor in an African American congregation in Los Angeles described how his understanding of a calling to serve in a support capacity helped him deal with other people's expectations.

> It truly is a calling to be in support ministry. People have said to me recently, "You could pastor. Why don't you pastor? Why don't you call the bishop and tell him that you need to pastor?" And I've told them, you know, "God has called me into this position." It's critical that we recognize the calling component. God can call us into the next level, too. And it's not about capability. It really is about God's direction. Not anything else, but God's direction. And I've told people when God tells me to do the next thing, that's when I will do it, and not a moment sooner.

This sense of "oughtness" can also lead to our recognizing the need to leave a position that is changing. A youth pastor described his experience of being asked to change his ministry focus at his church.

> The pastor said the youth ministry was going well, but what the church needed now was an associate pastor who could preach, counsel, and do visitation. He asked me to move into that position, but I declined because my sense of calling to youth ministry was so strong. I ended up looking for a new church to serve and left within the year. They got their associate pastor, and I got to continue in youth ministry.

In these examples, and many others we heard and read, the sense of secret call was critical to an associate staff member's perseverance and decision making in ministry.

The Providential Call: Growth through Service

The third aspect of calling is the "providential call" of God, guiding a person through life in a way that he or she gains the experiences and gifts needed for vocational ministry.[4] John Newton, the former slave trader who wrote the hymn "Amazing Grace," served as a pastor for sixteen years. During this time, in 1765, he responded to a request from a man asking how to discern God's call to be a pastor:

> The main difference between a minister and a private Christian seems to consist in these ministerial gifts which are imparted to him, not for his own sake, but for the edification of others. But then I say, these are to appear in due season; they are not to be expected instantaneously, but gradually, in the use of proper means. They are necessary for the discharge of the ministry, but not necessary as prerequisites to warrant our desires after it.[5]

Newton took the aspect of providence in one's calling further, looking at how God not only prepares the individual for vocational ministry but also provides the opportunity to minister.

> That which finally evidences a proper call is a correspondent opening in Providence, by a gradual train of circumstances pointing out the means, the time, the place, of actually entering upon the work of the ministry. And until this coincidence arrives, you must not expect to be always clear from hesitation in your own mind.

No matter one's inner experience or sense of calling, God must provide the opportunities to serve and to grow in the work of ministry. These experiences confirm the inner experience of the secret call.

The Ecclesiastical Call: Confirmation from the Church

The fourth type of call is the "ecclesiastical call"—a congregation (or other church body) affirms an individual's gifts and calling and invites him or her into a leadership role.[6] John Calvin spoke of this act as a corporate call, a recognition by the church of the person's gifts and God's calling for ministry, and then a setting apart of the individual for a particular service. Calvin stressed that the individual's secret call experience and the corporate call of the church serve a complementary function, confirming the call to vocational ministry. One educational ministry staff member describes his own experience at a time of great discouragement.

> When I left my position I was greatly discouraged, not knowing if I should continue in ministry in the church or not. When the pastor and board of the church I interviewed at extended their call to me, and affirmed how my gifts fit with what they were needing, it encouraged me to give it another try. That ministry experience was better, and God used it to confirm my calling. Even when I ended up leaving that church, they affirmed my calling to ministry leadership. That meant a lot.

How God's Call Helps Associate Staff Thrive

Veteran associate staff members who are thriving reflect on God's calling in the past and present and see how God directs and sustains them in their ministry. This review of their calling helps them thrive where they are, doing what they are doing, in a number of ways.

Providing Peace of Mind in Vocational Choice

People serving in associate staff positions in local churches are certainly capable of doing other kinds of work. Given the many choices before them and the limited pay that normally accompanies vocational ministry, having a strong, clear sense of calling helps give associate staff members peace of mind and confidence that this work is what they should be doing. It is important to know yourself, how God has gifted and called you. This knowledge can help associate staff members find contentment in ministry. For some who do leave vocational ministry, the call from God is so clear that they experience a lack of peace away from it and eventually return. For them, peace is found through realizing one's call. One music minister told of his experience of leaving church staff ministry for a time and the reason he finally returned to it.

> I think for those who are truly called, there is a burning desire to continue in that. I've been on both sides of the fence. I had difficulties in situations earlier in my life and I dropped out. But in those five years that I was not in the ministry, I found myself at the church constantly helping in music programs and that kind of thing, trying to get back into the thing that I knew God had called me to do. And there was a burning desire to do that. There is not anything I could do. I was happy with what I was doing, but I was not doing what I knew that I needed to do.

A children's pastor echoes this sentiment, describing her own struggle with leaving and returning to children's ministry.

> I would say number one [for thriving in ministry] is a strong sense of call. I don't think I can—in fact, I know I can't—do anything else, because I've tried. You know, I've jumped out of staff positions and church ministry and tried to do other things, but a sense of call is too strong. I cannot stay there without being miserable. I've got to go back to what I've been called to do.

Fueling Passion for and Perseverance in Ministry

Calling can also bring out a passion for ministry that stands strong in the face of adversity, a passion to see God's kingdom grow and to be a partner in ministry with Jesus Christ. Vocational ministry brings with it times of great stress as well as times of joy. Associate staff ministry is no exception. During times of stress, frustration, and adversity, having a strong sense of calling to ministry can help the associate staff member persevere instead of quitting. Calling that is tested by adversity drives the person to God in prayer, seeking the strength, wisdom, and courage to continue to face the challenges and minister faithfully. In this way, calling can strengthen one's faith and faithfulness. One director of Christian education explained how her passion for ministry grew out of her sense of calling and helped her weather a season of stress on the job.

> I have a real desire to be involved in kingdom work. When we went through a time where stress levels were high because of a conflict between the music minister and the senior pastor, the thing that kept me going was not the appreciation of the senior pastor. I didn't feel a real staff togetherness like I do now, but I still felt called to the kingdom of God and my passion to make a difference in people's lives, a strong love for people and my love for God that superseded all the tensions and other things that happened to be going on. I could hang in there through thick and thin as long as I feel like I'm in partnership with the Lord. He enables you to do things that, on your own, anybody else would throw up their hands and say, "I quit. I'm out of here, bud." And I had all kinds of people in the church ask me, "Why do you stay?" And it was easy for me to answer that, because I really feel like I'm looking for the Lord. I'm called by him. I feel a passion to be involved in kingdom ministry and to be a partner with Christ himself.

A minister of music also described how a sense of call enabled him and a colleague to weather a difficult time in their ministries.

> We recently have gone through a real radical change in our church. The minister of education and I sat many hours

contemplating the possibility of leaving the ministry or, at least, leaving the church but staying in ministry. We debated and came up with all the right reasons that it's OK to do it. But when we came back to the call, it was a totally different picture. We couldn't get past the fact that we're called to do this even when times are the toughest and you can't see past the next five minutes. That calling is what carries you through . . . for some who might call this a job, it's much more than a job.

Offering Joy and Fulfillment in Ministry

As people pursue the calling for ministry they have received from God, a deep satisfaction and joy can follow. An overwhelming 99 percent of the thriving associate staff in the original study, and 100 percent in our 2012 study, reported having a sense of fulfillment that comes from using their gifts to serve God in their ministry area. This does not mean that they never experience distress or discouragement, but as associate staff persevere through those times, God helps them find a joy and satisfaction again in the ministry that they can find nowhere else. One Christian education director who juggles many responsibilities in the congregation and who teaches at a Christian university describes how this has worked out in her life.

> Something that is really key for me is having a sense of God's call on my life–knowing this is what God wanted me to do and where God wanted me to do it. And that has been the overriding factor in my longevity, I believe, and that is my commitment to doing what I believe the Lord wants me to do. And then also loving, absolutely loving the church, the ministry, the people here, the pastor, and the tasks. I love Christian education. That's my slice of the pie. And as such, I'm responsible for all teaching ministries from children to adults. And I love training teachers and developing curriculum, and all that. That is really my forte, and I love doing that here.

Another associate staff member warns of the negative impact when a person takes on a ministry role that does not really fit his calling, leading to a lack of joy in the work.

Some of the worst cases I've observed are those pastors who accepted a job at a church because they didn't want to move or sell their current house or pull their kids out of a school. The church, more often than not, is a mismatch and the results are horrible. It is better to have a clear conscience about your calling.

Ensuring Contentment in Ministry

Our society encourages employees to move up the corporate ladder and become executives. Even in our congregations, associate staff members can sometimes feel pressure to "grow up" and become pastors of their own congregations. I don't know how many times I was asked the question, when will you become a senior pastor? and it was difficult to help some people understand that I was not called to that kind of ministry. This cultural expectation can exert subtle pressure on associate staff members, causing some to feel discontented with their current ministry positions. A strong and clear call can help an associate staff member face those pressures and that spirit of discontent and find real satisfaction in her ministry in the present, instead of anxiously looking forward to some change in the future. One youth pastor put it succinctly: "If you are called to minister to youth, there's no pressure to try to be a senior pastor." An associate pastor from Toronto warns of the dangers of losing this perspective.

> The younger generation is being trained more on the business model of looking at stepping-stones and career moves. "I will go to this church for two or three years and then, you know, I'll be able to step up." I really believe that biblically there is no basis for that. When you're called to a ministry, you should be called to that ministry until God chooses to call you out of it. So you don't set yourself up for "I'm here for a couple of years just to put in my time until I get something that I really want." If you have that mentality, you don't normally stay very long. And if you have that mentality, and you have your stepping-stone above what your expectations and giftedness are, you not only don't get there, you get out of the ministry. A lot of the people are out of the ministry because of those kinds of situations.

A Dynamic Call

Not everyone has the same kind of clarity, specificity, or stability to his or her calling to ministry. For some people it is a fairly general call to serve God's church, and the ways this call can be lived out change over time. From their understanding, God has called them to vocational ministry but has not made clear how this calling is to be fulfilled. An exploration of their ministry gifts and opportunities to work in various types of ministry eventually lead to an understanding of how they should minister, but this perception can change with time. For these people, there is no sense of *identity* as a particular type of minister (for example, youth pastor) but only as one who ministers. Changes in how this calling to minister is to be lived out are anticipated and viewed as normal.

Others experience their call as quite specific to an area or type of ministry, and they may view themselves as "lifers," totally committed to this particular kind of ministry. Such a calling brings a strong sense of identity and stability. For these people, God's call has a sense of permanence. They may agree that God is free to redirect them in the future, but they do not anticipate such an outcome. Any growth or development of this type of calling is seen as growth within one ministry field, not a move to a new and different ministry focus. Many, though not all, of the thriving long-term associate staff members described their sense of calling in this way.

Still others find that their call is to serve a particular congregation, and their ministry responsibilities change as the church's needs change. But even this may need to change. I have a friend with whom I played disc golf every week for several years. (If you're wondering what disc golf is, picture a par-three golf course where instead of hitting balls into a hole, you throw Frisbee-like discs at baskets on poles. That's pretty close!) Wayne served the same church for about twenty years in four different associate staff capacities: junior-high intern, children's pastor, executive pastor, and adult-ministries pastor. His desire is to follow God in service, and God has directed him to serve a specific church through a variety of means. Following these twenty years in one congregation, God directed him to a new church for service. What began as an investment within one congregation, God then turned into a new calling of service to a new group in need of his leadership.

All these experiences of God's calling have a dynamic element. Though God's call to ministry happens in time, it is not merely a historical event to look back on. God's call is a living reality that we live out. This means that for some people, their original understanding of calling grows over time. They learn through their ministry experiences, their dormant gifts blossom as opportunities arise to exercise them, and new demands draw out new passions for ministry. For others, the growth in their calling is a deepening that leads to new ways to live it out. For example, I know several wonderful youth-ministry professors who began as youth pastors in local churches. Their calling to youth ministry is still vital, but it has now become a ministry of reproduction, of equipping others for youth ministry leadership roles. In all these ways God is at work, confirming, enlarging, or redirecting the call to minister. It is important that we, as associate staff, remain open to follow God's guidance faithfully. As we do so, we will find that the living God is able to strengthen and sustain us in the ministries we carry out, walking us through the difficult times, guiding us when a change is needed, and helping us thrive in the process.

What If I Don't Feel Called?

As I have said, not everyone has the same experience of a calling, and some people may question whether they have indeed been called to vocational ministry. Others may believe that God called them in the past, but they wonder whether God still wants them in ministry. There is no easy way to determine a call, but we must take care not to make vocational changes too quickly. Many people experience God's call through a process of events, with greater clarity emerging as they are able to look back at how God has equipped and supported them in their ministries. One long-term children's ministry director described how her own sense of calling changed over the years and how that change has affected her perspective and passion for ministry.

> I think sometimes we hear, "I'm called." And that may be used
> loosely by some people, but I think that in children's ministry
> you are called. And if you're not, you don't last long term. For
> years I did the job. I started out, it was kind of like I was there,

you know, and they said, "Here, come do this." And I had never even taught Sunday school, and they wanted me to direct. And so for years I went through the motions. My husband was transferred, and we left and came to Dallas. And at that point, I said I would never work in another church because it was the busywork. It was all those things. And God just hit me over the head, and said, "No, I prepared you, and now I've called you." Now, I've been twenty-three years in ministry, but the last five, I believe I was really called and I'm finally connecting with the kids. And it is a passion. I live it. I eat it. I breathe it. You know, my husband thinks that he is number two. I try real hard to make him think he is not, but you know, really, I just want to serve God with the kids.

If you are wondering whether God has indeed called you to vocational ministry, take time to review the four aspects of calling described above, reflect on your ministry experience and your walk with God, and talk with fellow Christians who know you well to help you understand how God is working in the present and desires to direct you. Finding a spiritual director to help you assess your calling may prove helpful to some people.

I began this chapter by describing my own experience of wrestling with my call to associate staff ministry. After leaving my first church staff position, I accepted an unexpected invitation to work on staff in another congregation. Over the next few years God worked to strengthen and equip me for ministry and to confirm my calling to develop and lead educational ministries in the church. I worked with an approachable and supportive pastor and a wonderful group of committed and gifted lay leaders. I began to see how my gifts fit with my ministry focus and what I needed to learn to become more effective. God eventually led me to service in a third congregation, where I found great joy, excitement, and satisfaction in ministry. I couldn't think of anything else I would rather do, even during those times when everything seemed to be going crazy. My sense of thriving in ministry had not come right away, and over the years there were times when I seriously questioned whether I was doing the right thing, but God worked through these circumstances to help me grow to the point that I could thrive despite stressful circumstances.

Taking Inventory: Questions for Reflection and Discussion

Like the remaining chapters of this book, this one closes with questions for personal reflection or group discussion. In some chapters we
separate them into two groups, one for new associate staff members
or people preparing for associate staff ministry, another for veteran associate staff members. You may find it beneficial to take time alone to
think through these questions, making them a focus for prayer and reflection. It may also be helpful to discuss them in a group setting with
peers in ministry. You could encourage each other to work through
the questions and clarify what is important to each of you, and what
responses, if any, you wish to make. For those who are married, discussing these questions with your spouse may be especially profitable.

Each person has a unique life and ministry situation, and these
questions may trigger other issues that would be more helpful for you
to consider. Use these questions in ways that will be of the most assistance to you. May you be granted clear discernment as you seek
to know God's direction for your life and ministry, and may you find
deep satisfaction in following it.

For Those in Preparation for Ministry or Newer Associate Staff Members

1. Secret Call: Would you say that God has *called* you to vocational
   ministry? How would you describe your inner sense of secret
   call? Have you shared this with anyone? How did they respond?
2. Providential Call: Looking back, how has God guided and
   equipped you for vocational ministry? What smaller steps and
   opportunities did God use to stretch and grow you and to give
   you a taste of what ministry involvement would be like?
3. Ecclesiastical Call: How has your own sense of calling been confirmed through the response of the church?
4. Focus of Calling: How would you describe to a friend the nature
   of your calling to ministry and the scope or focus of that calling?
   If you have not shared this with someone, select someone with
   whom to talk about this who would be interested in supporting
   you as you pursue this calling.
5. If you are wondering whether your calling is to vocational ministry, with whom might you be able to talk and pray in order to

begin to sort this out and to understand more clearly what God desires for your life?

For Veteran Associate Staff Members

1. Have you seen God expand or redirect your call to ministry over time? If so, in what ways has it changed? If you have any sense of what may lie ahead for you, where do you see God taking you in ministry in the years to come?
2. In the past, how has your calling by God helped you survive the demands of ministry? If there have been times when you felt you were not thriving, in what ways did your sense of calling help you?
3. Are you now experiencing difficulties in your ministry that are discouraging? If so, take time to review your call from God into ministry. Make this a focus for prayer, and ask God to reaffirm or redirect your calling and to provide the strength, guidance, and courage needed to persevere in your situation as long as necessary.
4. If you are wondering if you are still called to vocational ministry, with whom might you be able to talk and pray in order to begin to sort this out and to understand more clearly what God desires for your life?

2

Sustaining Spiritual Vitality in Ministry

My soul clings to the dust;
give me life according to your word!

—PSALM 119:25

Of all the advice on how to thrive offered by veteran associate staff members in this study to those just beginning, the most frequently mentioned was taking time to nurture and maintain personal spiritual vitality. It seems that for real thriving in ministry, *nothing* is as foundational as the quality of our own relationship with God. Thriving has more to do with personal spiritual well-being than with the circumstances of our ministries. While our work contexts can make ministry goals easier or harder to achieve, they will not ensure an ability to thrive. But when we cultivate an intimate relationship with the God who has called us to ministry, we have a resource to sustain us through the ups and downs of our circumstances. God is able to provide grace to meet the challenges of life and ministry, peace of mind and heart in times of trouble, and joy and deep satisfaction as we see God's purposes accomplished in and through the church.

Unfortunately, our ministerial vocation does not ensure that our own souls will receive the ongoing nurture and care we need. The constant demands associate staff members face can crowd out the time and attention that should be given to our own spiritual growth. It is easy to feel that because we are preaching, teaching, or counseling others, we ourselves must be growing spiritually. But studying the Bible to preach or teach others does not ensure that we are opening our own hearts to God's instruction and molding. Praying for the needs of others does not necessarily mean that we are dealing with our own spiritual needs. And devoting our efforts to helping others to know and walk with God does not guarantee that we are walking along with them. Eugene Peterson, author of many books on ministry issues and of *The Message: The Bible in Contemporary Language* version of the Bible, shares this warning in his book on vocational holiness, *Under the Unpredictable Plant:* "In our eagerness to be sympathetic to others and meet their needs, to equip them with a spirituality adequate to their discipleship, we must not fail to take with full seriousness our straits, lest when we have saved others we ourselves should be castaways."[1]

I (Kevin) know how easy it is to neglect my own spiritual growth while serving in ministry. Over the eleven years that I served on church staff, I frequently struggled to give adequate attention to my own spiritual nurture. Many times I was so busy providing opportunities for others to come to the spiritual banquet table and enjoy the feast that all I took time for were some bread crusts eaten on the run. Fortunately for me, God did not allow me to continue on that way for long. God used people I worked with; times of worship with the congregation; conversations and prayer with my wife, Patty; ministry and family crises; and the Word itself to reawaken my need and hunger for a closer, vital relationship. Without this ongoing spiritual renewal, thriving deteriorates to surviving as we go through the motions of ministry, turning our vocations into jobs to be done.

Fortunately, veteran associate staff members have found many ways to nurture their own spiritual growth in the midst of ministry demands. They describe a foundational attitude and a variety of spiritual disciplines that have been beneficial for their own spiritual vitality and which have helped them thrive in ministry.

Cornerstone: An Attitude of Humility and Openness

The starting place for all spiritual growth is an attitude of humility before God and an openness to the Holy Spirit's working in our lives to transform us toward the image of Jesus Christ. Our awareness of our ongoing need for God's involvement in our lives and our willingness to seek God amid life's demands are foundational for any spiritual growth.

One danger for those in vocational ministry is losing our focus on God's guidance, strength, and grace and beginning to focus on our own abilities, skills, and accomplishments. Pride is an occupational hazard as we receive words of praise and appreciation from others about how our ministry has benefited them. Our studies and ministry experience can lure us into a false sense of security and capability. If we are not careful, our sense of dependence on God can fade, leaving us trying to do what only God can do. A youth pastor puts it simply and well:

> You keep humble and you keep growing. It's very easy to get a messiah complex. Like it's not going to work unless I do it. That is an enormous trap, not just for any youth pastor but for any senior pastor to fall into. We just need to keep humble.

A commitment to humility and to seeking God first in our lives and ministries calls us to develop a close walk with God. This relationship can be nurtured in many ways, and thriving associate staff members share a number of practices that have been helpful for them. Whatever approaches are used, the focus is on knowing God and being open to the love and direction God provides so that our lives and ministries can be faithful to divine purposes. Another youth pastor described the power of this growing relationship with God for his ministry:

> It's my own personal relationship with Christ that renews me. You're up and down, but if I wasn't doing it for Christ, I would have been gone long ago. If that relationship was not built on a regular basis, there would be no way that I could be involved in doing what I've done, because of all the stuff that you have to put up with. To me that's the number-one reason that I keep going on, that relationship that burns every day, that you want to spend time with him. And the strength comes from that.

This foundational attitude keeps us open to God's work in our lives, helping us benefit from a variety of foundational spiritual practices.

Foundational Practice 1:
Prayer for Personal Growth and Ministry Guidance

One basic foundation for personal spiritual vitality in ministry is spending regular times in conversation with God in prayer. Virtually all the associate staff in our studies who are thriving in their ministry efforts report that this is an important practice for them. Scripture calls us to an intimate time of talking with and listening to God in prayer. As we experience such communion, God provides peace to our souls. As Paul wrote, "Do not be anxious about anything, but in everything by prayer and supplication with thanksgiving let your requests be made known to God. And the peace of God, which surpasses all understanding, will guard your hearts and your minds in Christ Jesus" (Phil. 4:6–7).

Associate staff who are thriving in their ministries report that praying regularly, either by themselves or with others, has had a powerful impact on their longevity and satisfaction in ministry. Taking regular times for prayer, talking with God about your life situation and what you are learning or need to learn, and being quiet before God are critical for ongoing direction in ministry and for personal growth. One youth pastor put it quite simply:

> I know it sounds like a cliché, but my own quiet times are critical. It's a roller coaster. There are ups and downs, but there have been seasons of really rich times in the Word and just being quiet where the Lord has refreshed me. And if you don't have that, you are going to dry up. It is as simple as that.

Another associate pastor described his own experience of the value of personal prayer time, and how he had difficulty at times defending his use of time to others.

> In church you are always praying with people, in staff meetings you are praying, but it's my own personal seasons of prayer . . . especially when I feel like I'm getting dry, I up the ante on the amount of time that I can pray. I incorporate the Word in that prayer time, letting the Word drive it. To me it's been in prayer time where I really get grounded and sense God's direction and his pleasure and his forgiveness, and his fuel for ministry. The renewal side of it is really getting away, setting that time to have an extended time of prayer (an hour or more). And you have to resist the pressure you can get from other pastors or other people who think that is a waste of time. . . . For me, that is when I'm feeling the fullest spiritually.

Many veteran associate staff also report that they have a prayer partner or a small group of people with whom they pray, which is a great encouragement to them. This relationship and prayer support help them to weather the demands of ministry. Some pray with a fellow staff member or a group of staff colleagues. One director of Christian education described how this practice came about on her staff: "When I came on staff we didn't have regular prayer times together. And so I and the youth minister, over a period of a couple of years, just forced it into our schedules. And now we're praying together twice a week."

Others pray with their spouse, a member of the congregation, or a small group they attend within the congregation. Still others have a friend, mentor, or group of peers outside the church that they share and pray with regularly. Another director of Christian education explained how she took time regularly with her prayer partners. "One of my prayer partners and I just plan a good part of the day in prayer and fasting every two or three months, and that helps a lot. Most of the time we spend alone, and then we compare what God has said to us."

Whatever the setting and whoever the companion, having someone who can listen to our needs, confessions, concerns, and joys and pray with and for us is a great help. For ministry longevity and for personal spiritual vitality, it is important that we have people we can and do pray with.

Foundational Practice 2:
Studying Scripture for Personal Growth, Not Just for Others

Another basic foundation for personal spiritual vitality is spending time listening to God through reading and studying Scripture. Most staff members are involved in Bible study as part of their ministry responsibilities. It can be easy to fall into a pattern of studying the Bible for others, reading it with an eye for how it applies to those we are teaching. Many times I felt as if my time studying Scripture to develop curriculum for use in an adult class or youth group was adequate for my own growth. However, if this is all we do, it is easy to miss God's message for us and to mistake familiarity with Scripture for personalized knowledge of its truth and power. The vast majority of associate staff members in our studies report that personal Bible study is an important investment for their ability to thrive in ministry. Two associate staff members with different ministry responsibilities described how important studying Scripture is for their own growth:

> You've got to keep growing spiritually. I know sometimes it's easy to say, "Well, I'm in the Bible all the time." But when you look at it, you're studying for this night's Bible study or preparing for this other thing. I need that spiritual growth personally. So I try to set aside a time where I'm not studying this because of the group or whatever. I'm studying this because I need to grow and I need to keep in touch with God and have that relationship.
>
> —A YOUTH PASTOR

> If I don't have a quiet time first thing in the morning, the first thing I do, I won't have it. There is a commitment that I have to sit down with God first thing in the morning and spend time in the Word, and spend time in prayer, and if I give myself enough time I allow myself time to meditate on God's Word, . . . I really spend time just soaking in the Word of God. And I think that, for me right now, where I am at, that is everything! It just keeps me going.
>
> —An ASSOCIATE PASTOR

As with prayer, many veteran associate staff report great benefits from participating in Bible study with a group of people, not just on their own. This time with others, without responsibility for leading the group, is a refreshing opportunity for personal growth. For many staff this happens best in a small-group Bible study context. Here they have the opportunity to participate with others in studying, discussing, and applying the message of Scripture to their lives. This is especially important for those who, like this children's ministry director, cannot attend the regular worship services of the church because of their own ministry responsibilities.

> It's important for me to go on Wednesday night to our Bible study at the church, because on Sunday morning I do not get

into the service. I get in for the music part with the special-
education class. In fact, very seldom do I get in to the preaching service. So Wednesday night is very important. I try very
hard to be sure that I am there.

Whether individually or with others, taking time to study God's
Word for personal application is a critical part of maintaining spiritual vitality in ministry. We cannot live off the Bible knowledge we
acquired in college or seminary. What we need is time to reread this
book that we think we know so well and allow the Holy Spirit to teach
us through the Word, showing us the relevance it has for our life situations and leading us in responding to God. Only then can our ministry
flow out of a vital walk with God and intimate experiential knowledge
of God's Word that shapes our own lives.

Foundational Practice 3:
Fostering Intimacy with God through Worship

Nurturing a vital relationship with God involves not only prayer and
Scripture reading but also worship. Whether privately or corporately,
our growing experience and knowledge of God stimulates a response
of worship and praise. If our prayer life focuses only on lists of requests, and the fruit of our Bible study is only a growing database of
biblical information or lessons for other people, then we are in danger
of spiritual anemia. For our relationship with God to grow in intimacy
and impact in our lives, we must take opportunities to spend time in
praise and worship.

Again, the vast majority of long-term associate staff members who
are thriving in their ministries report that they experience great intimacy with God in worship and that this factor helps them thrive in
ministry. This intimacy in worship is a source of strength and joy as
they carry out the responsibilities that come with their staff positions.
Its importance for spiritual vitality cannot be underestimated.

Meeting this need can be difficult for staff members whose responsibilities take them away from their congregation's regular Sunday morning worship services. For a time, it may be a workable
arrangement, but eventually the impact of the lack of participation
in corporate worship is felt. Cheryl, a children's ministry director,

started working at a church that had one morning worship service. Because of her work responsibilities, she was never able to attend the service. Later, when the church began holding two services, she still was tied up with work responsibilities and did not attend. For four years this pattern continued, and Cheryl found it to be more and more draining and discouraging. When the congregation finally decided to hire additional staff to work with Cheryl, it opened the opportunity for her to resume participating in corporate worship, which provided her spiritual encouragement and refreshment. Now, as the children's ministry staff has grown, Cheryl works with the schedule to ensure that each staff member has the opportunity to attend one of the worship services. She knows firsthand how important it is to maintain personal spiritual well-being in the midst of ministry demands.

Another children's pastor who could not attend Sunday morning worship services described how important singing was to her and how she found another opportunity for that type of worship experience:

> The worship service is really a high priority for me. I feel that it is also important for me to model this for the teachers I work with. I miss the singing part of the worship service, and that is hard for me. So I joined a gospel choir that meets midweek because I love the music. If I just go and sing on Wednesday night, I'm praising God and I love that. And if I get to sing with them in the jails and sing with them on Sunday morning, that's a plus.

Along with corporate worship, having times for individual worship is also important. Some associate staff describe how taking time outside in God's creation or listening to Christian music helps them worship God during the week. These times of reflection on God's greatness and goodness, and our response of thankful praise, help us declare the worthiness of God to receive glory and honor. Worship helps us keep a proper perspective on the God we serve and on ourselves as God's dependent children. This perspective helps us better evaluate and respond to the demands of life and ministry, keeping us from the traps of self-dependence and pride.

Other Spiritual Disciplines to Consider

Along with the three major spiritual disciplines described above, most thriving associate staff members have found a number of other disciplines to be helpful in nurturing a vital relationship with God. The percentage of thriving associate staff who report this has increased from 61 percent in 1998 to 95 percent in 2012. The listed disciplines are not exhaustive but represent the practices that many associate staff members have found to be beneficial for their own spiritual development and health. Not all are equally beneficial to everyone, so look these over to see which might be most beneficial for you.

Taking Personal Retreats

Almost half of the thriving associate staff in this study report that they periodically take extended time away from work, from part of a day to an overnight retreat, for prayer and personal spiritual renewal. These "mini-sabbaths" for spiritual re-creation are a helpful discipline for restoring perspective, resting, and allowing God to minister to us and guide us. These times apart can be an important tool for ongoing spiritual development in the face of heavy ministry demands. One youth pastor described how he uses mini-retreats to restore his vision for ministry.

> Periodically I take time away from the church, a couple [of] hours, sometimes three to five. Sometimes I go sit on the beach; sometimes I go up to the mountains. Sometimes I read God's Word for an hour and pray. Sometimes I may sit down and say, "God, I just need to pour out my heart to you. I need to pour out the vision that I'm feeling inside of me, but I don't know how to put it down, and I need to sit with you and deal with it right now in the quietness of the time I have here. I need to work through this with you."

Seeking Spiritual Direction

A smaller percentage of associate staff members have individuals they turn to as mentors or spiritual directors. These associates respect the spiritual maturity of their mentors and find great benefit in sharing their life situations with them, praying with them, and seeking wise counsel from them in spiritual matters. Whether one has a formal spiritual director or a more informal relationship with a mentor, having someone with spiritual maturity listen to our life stories and help us understand how God may be working, and what God desires of and for us, provides new perspective and encouragement to us.

Listening to Audio Recordings while Exercising or Driving

Like the rest of contemporary culture, associate staff members are aware of how important it is to stay healthy. We all receive advice to eat right, get plenty of sleep, and exercise. Also, many of us spend a bit of time on the road getting to and from our offices. Many of the associate staff members we talked with in our focus groups in 2012 reported that with their schedules being so busy, they find it helpful to use the time that they are exercising or driving for spiritual renewal as well. In an age where MP3 players are getting smaller and holding more files, it is easy to bring recordings of sermons, the Bible, audiobooks, blogs, and inspirational music into our exercise routine or into our cars, allowing our focus to be on spiritual renewal as we do other things. A few associate staff shared how they incorporate listening to spiritually encouraging recordings during their other activities.

> When I exercise, I listen to sermon podcasts. For whatever reason, that just gets me going. My life is incredibly busy, so it is not quiet unless I get up early in the morning and do this.

> Recently I've been taking my iPod to the gym and on the machine I've been reading through chapters of the New Testament. . . . I've been trying to read through ten chapters of the New Testament a day, which gets you through the whole New Testament in a month. I've been trying that because it is new and different. Don't just do the things you've always done. Maybe I can listen to a sermon, or an audiobook, or a podcast, or read the Bible on my iPod in the gym. We need to be open to new ideas and help spur one another on.

> Driving to and from the church gives me a little time when I can listen to praise music, sermons, Scripture recordings, and

good books to help me focus on God and prepare myself for the day. It's the only time I have where it is quiet and I can focus. Life at home is too hectic, and it's busy at the office. I love this time.

Journaling

Some long-term associate staff have found that keeping a prayer journal or pursuing some other form of journal writing is helpful for their spiritual growth. For some, the discipline of writing helps focus their thoughts for prayer or for better understanding the message of the Scripture passages they have been reading and reflecting on. A minister of Christian education explained how he combined journaling with his other devotional practices.

> I have found the one thing that has truly kept me going and kept my vision was meeting with God in his Word each morning and knowing what he said to me. Writing to the Lord has been helpful, responding to what he said to me in the Word that day, so that it's not just, "Well, I've read my Bible today." I know what God said to me, and that gives me the strength to go on.

Others find it helpful to write about their spiritual journey and reflect back on it at a later date to see how God is working and leading them. One youth pastor described the eclectic nature of his journal.

> One thing I do is journal a lot—my own personal joys and pitfalls and struggles. I have a spiral binder that's my journal. Yesterday, someone said, "So how is it organized?" I said, "Organized? It's not organized." It's just kind of there, and if I'm feeling something, I'll sit down and spend some time writing. I have letters to my son in there, I have sermon notes in there, but it's kind of my spiritual journey. Just a couple of days ago, on my birthday, I spent some time looking back at the past couple of years of journal entries on or near my birthday. It's an incredible process to look through that and go, "Whoa, I can see those up years and those down years, those up times

and those down times." And I can see the faithfulness of God
in all of it.

Whether organized or not, writing in a journal has been of benefit
to many in focusing their thoughts on how God is at work in their
lives, both to transform them into Christ's image and to use them in
ministry in the church.

Serving in Cross-cultural Settings

Some associate staff find that getting involved in ministry in a cross-
cultural setting is a stimulus to their spiritual growth. Moving outside their comfort zones, talking with others about how God is at
work in their lives, seeing and experiencing the needs of others,
and working with others to respond to those needs open their eyes
to see God's work in the world in new ways. The experience gives
them a profound appreciation of God's grace to their churches and
new visions of how God wants to use them and others in ministry. A
youth pastor explained how cross-cultural ministry was a discipline
for him, something he did intentionally to keep growing in his walk
with God.

> You need to keep putting yourself in different experiences and
> different places as well as do your usual ministry. For example,
> going on the missions trips and getting in the ditch with a kid
> and be willing to do that kind of work. We're just back from
> Russia, and with each mission trip you take, it changes your life.

Keeping Sabbath Rest

One occupational hazard for people in vocational ministry is the
heavy work demands they face on Sunday, a traditional "Sabbath,"
or day of rest. While many Christians may be able to take Sunday
as a day for worship, rest, and recreation, most associate staff members find this to be the busiest day of their week. Some long-term
associate staff members who are thriving in their ministries report
that they intentionally schedule other sabbaths into their schedules,
not just for physical rest but also for spiritual renewal. A women's

ministry director described how this practice had recently become important for her.

> I have been really convicted for the past two or three months of my need to have a sabbath. I just have not taken that commandment seriously. I love Sunday, but it's my busiest day of the week. So, to take another day out and have a sabbath is needed. I think, this is stupid, but I think I operate under the paradigm that if I'm not working somehow, God is not working. Isn't that arrogant? It's like the height of arrogance. But for me to actually say, "Now, I'm not going to work on this day." So, that's been key for me to take Friday or Saturday as a sabbath. I'm still trying to figure out all of what that means, but I know it means that I don't work.

Taking weekly sabbaths can help renew the energy needed to tackle the problems that come in ministry, helping you avoid burnout. A youth pastor stressed the importance of this renewal for him.

> I find that if I'm not taking regular times, like on a weekly basis, to have a sabbath, then the little problems seem to get accentuated somehow, and then something that isn't so big seems huge. So I find just in terms of personal maintenance that having a weekly sabbath, where you just don't do anything, is important. It's a time of rest, of solitude, listening, reading, praying.

It is not always easy to get this sabbath time away, and some associate staff, like this children's pastor, have had to take some radical steps to create the boundaries needed for genuine rest.

> I keep my day off as my day off. I don't answer phone calls, I don't check my e-mail. I don't go into the office for a minute, I don't do anything. I play with my kids. . . . I let [the phone] go to voice mail if it is church and I will check it, because I don't have to talk to a person. Every couple of months we take a few days and I won't even go to that church. If I take a week off, I go to a different church just so I can worship and not have someone come up and pester me.

Seeking Fellowship

Because associate staff members carry significant ministry responsibilities, and much of their contact with congregation members re-
volves around ministry needs and planning, it can be easy for them to
miss out on the benefits of a rich fellowship with others in the church.
Some thriving associate staff intentionally find fellowship opportunities within their churches where they can relax and participate with
others instead of being in charge. A children's ministry director explained how this experience was important for her.

> We have a group we call "Twenty-something." I go to it on
> Sunday nights. I get my name tag just like everybody else. I
> usually show up late just because I can, and it's so refreshing.
> It's also a little strange to not be in supervision of this group. I
> don't know what they're speaking on a month from now, so it's
> a little strange for me. The fact that it's strange only reinforces
> that I really need to be there.

Maintaining Accountability to Others

Another discipline that some associate staff members have found
helpful for their own spiritual growth is participation in a support
and accountability group. (This kind of supportive fellowship will
be discussed in more detail in a later chapter.) Having a person or a
group of people to whom they are accountable and with whom they
can share the struggles of their spiritual journey is a tremendous
encouragement. It helps them stay honest with themselves and challenges them to follow God closely in all that they do. A women's
ministry pastor said this kind of accountability was difficult but beneficial to her.

> I stay submitted to others. Yesterday, I and my staff had a
> prayer time. I had to confess to them something the Lord had
> really been dealing with me about. I had to lay it out there so
> they could hold me accountable to it. That's hard, but not do-
> ing it is harder.

Spiritual Vitality and the Woman Associate Staff Member

While similar percentages of men and women associate staff members have spiritual disciplines that strengthen their faith and their relationship with God, women more than men reported that their regular participation in spiritual disciplines is influential in their ability to thrive in ministry. Women also said they valued, more than men did, having their supervisor encourage their spiritual growth and well-being. In general, more women than men reported the practice and value of spending extended times away in prayer (retreats). While more men reported the practice of regular Bible study for personal growth, more women than men rated it as influential in their ability to thrive in ministry. The reasons for these differences are not clear. The survey results may reflect the impact of a more stressful ministry setting for women and a heightened awareness of the need for God's strength and guidance, but there is no hard evidence to back up this hypothesis. The findings may also reinforce a perception of women as more spiritually attuned, valuing the meditative practices of prayer and retreats more than men do. Again, the reason is not clear.

Whatever the explanation for this difference, it seems important for women associate staff members to develop and engage regularly in spiritual disciplines that nurture their spiritual vitality and growth, treating this practice as integral to their ministries, not just an exercise done when one has free time. How are you keeping such disciplines in the midst of your family and ministry demands? Which disciplines are most beneficial to your spiritual vitality? Are you shortchanging your own spiritual health in the name of ministry productivity? From what we learned from other women associate staff, your spiritual growth must become a priority for your long-term health and well-being in ministry.

Dryness and Discouragement with God

Do people who are thriving in associate staff ministry ever feel spiritually dry or discouraged? Yes! That seems to be a common experience of Christians in general, and people in vocational ministry are no exception. While this chapter has focused on the ways that associate staff members can sustain their spiritual vitality, there is no magic formula or set of activities for making this happen. Anyone who has read the Psalms sees that life brings with it times of sorrow, pain, and discouragement. While discouragement in your ministry can be difficult to deal with, your own spiritual dryness and discouragement with God can be even more difficult. If not faced and resolved, this condition will eventually make ministry more and more draining, causing some to leave vocational ministry or to turn it into just a religious job.

Eugene Peterson describes his own experience early in ministry that drove him to seek a spirituality adequate for his calling both as a Christian and as a minister.

> In my thirtieth year and four years into my ordination, an abyss opened up before me, a gaping crevasse it was. I had been traveling along a path of personal faith in Jesus Christ since childhood; in adulthood and entering my life work, the path widened into an Isaianic highway in the wilderness, a vocation in gospel ministry. Who I was as a Christian was now confirmed and extended in what I would do as a pastor. I and my work converged: my work an extension of my faith, vocation serving as paving to make the faith accessible for others who wished to travel this road.
>
> Then this chasm opened up, this split between personal faith and pastoral vocation. I was stopped in my tracks. I looked around for a bridge, a rope, a tree to lay across the crevasse and allow passage. I read books, I attended workshops, I arranged consultations. Nothing worked.
>
> Gradually it dawned on me that the crevasse was not before but within me. Things were worse than I had supposed; this was requiring more attention than I had planned on. Unwilling, finally, to stand staring indefinitely into the abyss (or loosen my grip on either faith or vocation, options that also occurred to me), I entered the interior territory in which the split had originated and found heavily eroded badlands. I searched for the details of discontinuity between my personal faith and my church vocation. Why weren't things fitting together simply and easily? I was a pastor vocationally; I was a Christian personally. I had always assumed that the two, "pastor" and "Christian," were essentially the same thing and naturally congruent. Now I was finding that they were not. Being a Christian, more often than not, seemed to get in the way of working as a pastor. Working as a pastor, with surprising frequency, seemed to put me at odds with living as a Christian.

Like Dives in hell, I was genuinely astonished. I had presumed that the life I had been living personally would issue vocationally into something blessed. Here I was experiencing instead "a great chasm . . . fixed" (Luke 16:26). Like Dives, I began praying "have mercy upon me, and send Lazarus to dip the end of his finger in water and cool my tongue" (Luke 16:24). Unlike Dives, I received relief–but not in a moment, and not without unaccountably long stretches of badlands waiting. Gradually, and graciously, elements of vocational spirituality came into view. The canyons and arroyos were not so much bridged as descended, and in the descent I reached a bottom from which I could ascend as often as I descended (but only after the descent) with a sense of coherence, the personal and the vocational twinned.

Exploring this territory and praying this prayer, I looked for a spirituality adequate to my vocation. Now, thirty years later, I am ready to give witness to the exploration and the prayer. I do it with considerable urgency, for I come across pastor after pastor standing bewildered before the same or a similar abyss. Sadly, many turn back, abandoning their ordained vocation for a religious job. I don't want any of these men and women, whom I count my colleagues and friends, to turn back. . . . Every time one of our company abandons this essential and exacting work, the vocations of all of us are diminished.[2]

If Peterson's experience of dryness sounds similar to your own, recognize that God is at work and is willing to bring you through the inner chasms you face. You are called to seek God, to be open to the Spirit's work, so that you may be brought through the chasms and back up to higher ground. Make your spiritual growth and vitality a priority, and as God nurtures your soul, your ministry will flow out of God's work in you, blessing you and those you minister with and to.

Taking Inventory: Questions for Reflection and Discussion

While sustaining personal spiritual vitality is foundational to thriving in ministry, you can pursue this vitality in many ways. Prayer, Bible study, and worship are the major disciplines that thriving associate staff members report as beneficial. Many other approaches can also be helpful. Whether you are just getting started or have been in vocational ministry for many years, the importance of this issue and the benefit of these practices are the same. As you read the questions that follow, take time to reflect prayerfully on them, or discuss them with someone who can listen and help you identify what responses could be most beneficial for you. May they be a stimulus to a closer walk with Christ in ministry.

Starting Right: A Few Questions for New and Future Associate Staff Members

1. Prayer Practices

   As you look at your current prayer life, do you find that you are taking adequate time to have good quality communication with God? If not, what is crowding it out? Ministry demands tend to increase over time, so making this a priority in your schedule must happen now, not be delayed until later. Is prayer something you look forward to, or does it feel more like a social obligation that has lost its meaning and joy? If it feels rushed, is there a way to carve out and take advantage of a better time in your schedule for prayer? Would it help to recruit a prayer partner or small group you could meet with on a regular basis to share and pray together? Would it help to try an occasional short prayer retreat away from the office? If you are married, how might your spouse be of help in praying for and with you?

2. Personal Study of Scripture

   Other than any study that you are doing for teaching or curriculum development responsibilities, are you making time to read and study the Bible for your own life? Are you taking time regularly for devotional reading in Scripture that allows the Holy Spirit to use it to teach and guide you? If Scripture is the primary way that God speaks to us in the present, how are you making it a priority in your life? Devotional patterns need to be set early in ministry, ensuring their continuation in the midst of heavy ministry demands. Would it help to find some devotional or Bible discussion-guide materials that you can use as a structure for your own study? Would it help to begin opening the Bible for personal study before you open your computer in the morning?

3. Worship Practices

If your future or new ministry demands make it difficult to be in worship services on a regular basis, what other options will you need to consider to keep corporate worship a part of your life pattern? Are there alternate services that you can attend or a small-group worship time you can participate in? You may need to discuss these ideas with your ministry supervisor to see what is possible. On a personal level, is there music you can listen to that may encourage expressions of thanks and praise to God? Can you take time outside to enjoy God's creation and let it be a stimulus to your praise? In your Bible study, can you take time to respond to God in prayer, giving thanks for what you have learned through the Word?

Continuing Well: A Few Questions for Veteran Associate Staff Members

1. Resolving Internal Tensions

Eugene Peterson reported that after a few years in vocational ministry he saw a chasm opening up in front of him and found a growing tension between the demands of serving as a pastor and following Christ. Do you find that kind of tension in your own life and ministry? Do the demands of ministry make caring for your own spiritual growth difficult? Who might you talk with about these inner tensions?

2. Prayer Practices

As you look at your current prayer life, do you find that you are taking adequate time to have good quality communication with God? Has this been squeezed due to your ministry schedule? Is prayer something you look forward to, or does it feel more like a social obligation that has lost its meaning and joy? If it feels rushed, is there a way to carve out and take advantage of a better time in your schedule for prayer? Would it help to recruit a prayer partner or small group you could meet with on a regular basis to share and pray together? Would it help to try an occasional short prayer retreat away from the office? If you are married, how might your spouse be of help in praying for and with you?

3. Personal Study of Scripture

   Other than any study that you are doing for teaching or curriculum development responsibilities, are you making time to read and study the Bible for your own life? Are you taking time regularly for devotional reading in Scripture that allows the Holy Spirit to use it to teach and guide you? Are you resting on biblical knowledge gained in the past instead of seeking God through Scripture in the present? If Scripture is the primary way that God speaks to us in the present, how are you making it a priority in your life? Would it help to be part of a Bible study group that you don't lead? Would it help to find some devotional or Bible discussion-guide materials that you can use as a structure for your own study? Would it help to begin opening the Bible for personal study before you open your computer in the morning?

4. Worship Practices

   Are you able to attend worship regularly in your church? If not, are there alternate services that you can attend or a small-group worship time you can participate in? In what ways are you encouraging yourself to worship God throughout the week? Is there music you can listen to that may encourage expressions of thanks and praise to God? Can you take time outside to enjoy God's creation and let it be a stimulus to your praise? In your Bible study, can you take time to respond to God in prayer, giving thanks for what you have learned through the Word?

Other Spiritual Disciplines to Consider

Taking personal retreats. Have you thought about taking time for a personal retreat for spiritual renewal? Where could you go? What scheduling would have to be done to free up time? What about a half-day retreat? Who would have to approve it? Would your congregation help with expenses for this kind of activity? What would you like to do with the time?

Seeking spiritual direction. Whom have you gotten to know whom you respect for wisdom and spiritual maturity? Would one of these people be open to meeting with you to serve as a spiritual counselor? If this kind of person is not nearby, to what extent would it still be beneficial to write, call, or e-mail to begin to talk about what God is doing in your life and the ways you are being challenged to grow? Is this the kind of relationship you would like to pursue at this time?

Listening to audio recordings while exercising or driving. Do you find that you have a lot of time in the car or at an exercise facility, where you could be listening to recordings of music, Scripture, audiobooks, or sermons? Why not try out listening to something that encourages your spirit and helps you focus on God and be attentive to his Spirit?

Journaling. Have you ever tried keeping a prayer journal or a journal in which you write what is happening in your life and what God is teaching you? If you have, but have not done so in some time, would this be a helpful discipline to try again? If you have not, consider trying it for a few days to see if it helps you attend more closely to the state of your soul and what God is doing and teaching you. If you have kept a journal in the past, take time to reread what you have written, and allow God to help you see how you have grown in the past and ways in which God may want to direct you in the present.

Serving in cross-cultural settings. Have you ever participated in a mission project or other ministry in another cultural setting? How did that experience affect you? What did you learn from it about yourself, others, or God? If you have not had this type of ministry experience, what opportunities are there for you to pursue one? Can you get approval to take time for this kind of service? Can you see benefit to you that you could share with those who would have to give their approval?

Keeping sabbath rest. If Sunday is a busy day for you in ministry, what other time during the week could serve as a time of sabbath rest for you? Do you feel that you already have adequate time for rest? If not, in what ways could your schedule be adjusted to carve out and protect the time? What would you do with this time if you could have it?

Seeking fellowship. Do you participate in a fellowship group that you do not have to lead? If not, is there an informal group of people you get together with regularly that functions similarly? Is a group available that you could consider attending? Is scheduling a problem? If so, can schedule adjustments be made to free you to attend?

Maintaining accountability to others. Do you have a person or small group of people with whom you share openly and who can help you be accountable in your walk with God? If not, whom do you know that you would like to do this with?

Dealing with Dryness and Discouragement

Are you at a point in your life where your spiritual life feels stunted or dried out? Is this primarily a result of a stressed lifestyle and feeling physically or emotionally worn out? If so, an upcoming chapter on balance in life and family (chapter 4) may help. If the dryness or discouragement you feel has other causes, you may want to consider finding someone you respect with whom to talk it over, to see if he or she can help you understand what lies behind your feelings. Recognize that this is a common experience, and God may have much to teach you if you will persevere. If you have never read Eugene Peterson's book *Under the Unpredictable Plant: An Exploration in Vocational Holiness,* quoted earlier, it could be a good place to start in examining the origins of your dryness and what might help you through it. Also, consider recruiting a friend or two in ministry to read and discuss the book together. You may find that you are able to encourage and support each other in the process of spiritual renewal.

3

Weathering the Stresses of Ministry over Time

And let us not grow weary of doing good, for in due season we will reap, if we do not give up. —GALATIANS 6:9

Even when we are convinced of God's call to vocational ministry and follow it and we participate in spiritual disciplines to nurture our own spiritual life with God, the demands and stresses of ministry can wear on us, discourage us, potentially incubating a spirit of disappointment or cynicism within us. Ministry leadership brings its own challenges to our spiritual vitality and sense of well-being, and we need to be aware of ways to weather through them well. Veteran associate staff members who thrive throughout their years of service have learned to give attention to some other practices that help maintain their sense of thriving in ministry in the midst of ministry stresses. First, they have learned to rejoice in their ministry successes and savor them, allowing these to be a source of encouragement, satisfaction, and motivation to continue in the face of current difficulties. Second, they have learned some specific ways to handle tough times and deal with discouragement, criticism, and conflicts.

Sources of Joy in Ministry

For people in associate staff positions, regardless of their ministry responsibilities, few experiences are as satisfying and motivating as seeing positive results in the lives of those to whom they minister. Seeing that their ministry is bearing fruit in the lives of others confirms their calling and assures them that God is able to use their gifts and efforts.

It is also rewarding to see that what they value and have given their lives to achieve is coming about. This realization is the source of their greatest joys in ministry.

Sharon, for example, has served as a children's pastor in her church for almost fifteen years. She has given and received more hugs, wiped more noses, and talked with more parents than she can remember. Each year, there are challenges, some bigger than others. Recruiting and training volunteers, planning Christmas events and vacation Bible school, meeting with teachers and program leaders, finding replacement teachers on Sunday morning–these tasks can eventually take it out of you. Many times over the years, especially lately, Sharon has felt worn down, just plain tired. When crises hit at times like that, she can feel discouraged. She sometimes wonders if she should resign and turn the position over to someone else. When this mood hits, she does two things to lift her spirits and renew her energy for ministry. First, she makes sure that she gets to spend time with the children, talking with them, exchanging hugs, enjoying their presence. At her church, punch is served to the children every Sunday, so she heads over to the table and starts pouring punch and talking with the kids. Second, she pulls out her "fuzzies" file and looks at pictures and reads cards and notes written to her by children and parents over the years. God uses these two things to restore her joy in ministry and to allow her to savor it.

Joys in ministry come in many shapes and forms and from many sources. When thriving associate staff were asked about their sources of joy in ministry, they cited these kinds of experiences.

Children's Pastors

When you walk into a room of children and they recognize you and stop crying.

Watching children you worked with grow up and graduate from high school.

Some of the children I had twenty years ago are now grown, and some of those are involved in ministry, and that makes me motivated. It's really exciting whenever you go to the altar to pray and one of those twenty-year-olds comes up to pray and to affirm what you are doing, as well as what they are doing. That's a real breathtaking thing now.

Going into a grocery store and suddenly hearing, "Debbie, Debbie, Debbie!" I turn around, and there is a van full of kids that come to our midweek program, bus kids. Out comes a mom I've never met, and I'm charged. That's a great moment, because I know there is a whole family potential now, and we've been trying to get to that.

Seeing a child make a commitment, and then watching them and seeing a change, and having a parent confirm it. That keeps me going a really long time.

Watching adults who come in with fear and trembling to be an assistant, and three years later they are running a whole department and they've found their niche, and they say to you, "Thank you for asking me to teach." That is cool!

The thing that brings me joy is when something works really well and I see the workers have joy working with the children.

Youth Pastors

For me, it's seeing kids become either volunteers or professional workers in the church as adults now. I don't think there's anything that gives me more joy.

The greatest thing is to somehow have confirmation back from the Lord that what you're doing is valuable, what you do matters, what you have done through the power of the Holy Spirit has increased the kingdom or made a difference in it. To be able to hold onto that is just the best.

Just seeing any progress in my kids at all! You've got your kids who are new to the group and they'll invite another friend, and that means a lot. And then you've got your person who is involved in youth ministry, but then they take steps to do deeper Bible study, or they graduate and come back after a

couple of years and they want to be on staff with you. Everyone is at different points, and if you can just monitor any type
of progression, it means the Lord is blessing and being merci-
ful. I'll go for that!

It's pure joy to me when you remember this twerpy little teen-
ager you just wanted to smack, one of the kind that just caused
nothing but grief and you invested a lot of time, energy, and
prayer over. And you're at a national youth gathering, and this
handsome adult walks up who is there with his five adult spon-
sors and thirty-five kids. And he says, "I wouldn't be here if it
wasn't for you." That's joy!

Educational Ministry and Discipleship Pastors

I get pleasure in seeing somebody benefit from a discipleship
group or a small group that I got started, something that they
feel really helped them.

Seeing people actually responding. Maybe on the basis of the
teaching or training you have done, you actually see them become more productive. I think that is really gratifying, because
that's what we are all about. Getting people equipped and actually seeing that person serve more effectively.

I've learned to really focus on my areas of giftedness. When I
do that, I find a lot more joy in ministry than if I allow myself
to be sucked into all the administrative details that are very
draining for me.

I just happen to have some kids in my college group now
whose parents were in my college group a long time ago. Seeing that come back around is a blessing.

This almost feels selfish, to see a young man or woman accept Christ and to see the light come on spiritually. Just to be
around it, you might not have had anything to do with it, but
just to be around and witness that. I can't put it into words—it's
better than a million dollars. To know that you have a purpose

in life that transcends making a buck, gaining respect, whatever ambitions you have. It makes up for the paychecks that aren't what you'd be making if you were teaching or whatever.

Music and Worship Ministers

I'm one of the most blessed people in the world because I have been able to take my two greatest loves, my love for the Lord and my love for music, and put them together, and that's my job. God has called me to help people really experience his presence in worship. Last Sunday, we were singing, and a lady in the front row had a tear come into her eye. I asked her after the service, "What happened in the service this morning?" She said, "I was so full of the presence of God I couldn't even sing anymore." One of the greatest joys of music ministry is to be able to see people really experience the presence of God.

My job is to equip people to do the work of ministry. And so whenever we see people succeed and get to the point where they can be ministers and are equipped to do that, that is very rewarding. People coming to know Christ and then being built up and equipped to do ministry, and then doing it.

A woman came to see me about her husband, who had problems singing, and she said, "See what you can do with Lawrence. He just can't carry a tune. He's just so embarrassing to me." Poor Lawrence was standing there, you know, six feet, two inches, this big, old guy. And I worked with Lawrence briefly. Then on Father's Day, there was Lawrence and his four sons in the Father-Son Choir. His face was just absolutely radiant. That's another moment of pure joy. It's just the times that you invest in people. When you see those seeds grow, it's such a blessing.

Associate Pastors

My joy comes out of seeing the joy in other people's lives. They discover who Christ is, and whether they become a teacher or discover a spiritual gift or ministry, they get involved in serving others. I think that's where my joy is, in seeing them being able to do that and find some sort of wholeness or completeness in that.

I'm behind a desk all week planning the ministry, but on Sundays I make a point of being at the punch table, serving those little cups of punch to the kids, and I'm talking to them and saying "Hi" to them. And my joy is when they come up and I feel those hugs around my legs, and they say, "Thanks for the birthday card." Or, "Guess what I did? I caught a fish this weekend." Those little things remind me why I'm here and what I'm doing.

Committee meetings are usually boring, but every once in a while when you see a committee look at a need or look at a possibility of a ministry and take a courageous step, whether it's money or what they are going to do to get out in front of an issue. Whether it's a need to be met or an opportunity to be taken, they are going to press forward, and it's not the staff. They are going to do it together. They're going to be right alongside you. Boy, when that happens, it's the "aha" moment. You know, we've grabbed this purpose together somehow. It's gotten out of the theology books and the Scriptures, and it's now living here in this group.

Reading over these types of comments, one sees a few common threads concerning joy in ministry for associate staff members.

Time: Some sources of joy take time to develop. Some fruits of our labors are not readily evident, but if we stay at it long enough, joy can come as we see how God works in the lives of those we have served.

Vicarious joy: Joy comes not just through our own ministries but also as those we have recruited, trained, and supported become fruitful in ministry. Much of our joy of ministry is vicarious as we see others in our ministry areas exercise their gifts.

People: Joy comes in our interaction with the people we serve, not in higher attendance numbers or higher levels of giving. It is change in the lives of people that brings joy. When people come to faith in Christ, grow to know God better, and follow in obedience in their daily lives, that is rewarding.

Multiplication: Joy comes when we see ministry come full circle, when those to whom we have ministered grow to the point that they begin to minister to others. This ministry multiplication is deeply satisfying.

Making a difference: Joy comes when we see that God has taken our gifts and passions for ministry and by grace has used them to make a difference in the kingdom.

Learning to Savor Ministry Joys

Since some joys of ministry can be fleeting experiences, thriving associate staff members have found ways to capture the moment and allow it to become a source of encouragement when their circumstances are not as pleasant. They intentionally find ways to remind themselves of the joys and successes of ministry during times of discouragement. Here are a few things they have found helpful that you may want to consider doing as well.

The "Joy" File

Many associate staff members have put together a file or box where they place thank-you notes, letters of encouragement, and other mementos of ministry highlights. When they begin to grow tired or discouraged in ministry, they open up that file or box and read through the contents, taking time to remember how God has worked in the past. This material becomes a source of encouragement as they face the demands of the present.

> I have this Tupperware box thing that I can't even put a lid on that I keep encouragement letters in. When I've had bad days, I'd reach in, "Man, where's that one note, where's that letter? Ahhh, OK." I know that sounds bad, because we should be getting our joy from the Lord, but still, that's where I was at. Now I can get a note and just stuff it in there, read it later, and go, "Thanks, God."
>
> —A YOUTH PASTOR

I find if someone writes something and gives it to me, that means so much. Lots of people say nice things, but just having something in writing enables me to savor what God is doing in and through me, and gives me something to read at times when I'm discouraged.

—An educational ministry pastor

I have a "fuzzies" file. I keep it in the front of my file drawer, in my desk. It's notes of encouragement that I've gotten from people, thank-you notes, cute little drawings from kids that I end up with. Sometimes I kind of journal on a piece of paper and throw it in there. When I get really discouraged and think, "Oh, it's going really bad," I pull it out and look through it and say, "There is joy in this."

—A children's pastor

The Picture Board

Because so much of the joy of ministry is related in some way to the people we serve, many associate staff members have found that keeping visual reminders handy of those they serve and work with is another way to remember what the ministry is all about, why it is important, and how God is working through them in the lives of others. Whether it is a photo album, a bulletin board of pictures and other mementos, or pictures drawn by children put on the office door, these visual reminders can be sources of encouragement and motivation in ministry.

Leading kids to Christ—I don't know anything that even comes close to matching it for joy. Probably the second place would be as I pass them on to the subsequent years in high school to see them faithfully serving and to see them be an integral part of the next program up. That's important. And the way I preserve it, I never take down kids' pictures. Our youth room is littered with pictures of people who used to be there too, because it's a constant reminder of praying for those kids and seeing where they are at.

—An educational ministries pastor

I have a drawer full of knickknacks from kids I have had in my youth group. Every now and then I'll open it up and paw through them. It can make me a little sad because I miss them, but it is a great encouragement as I think back on all we did together and how they have grown.

—A YOUTH PASTOR

Anniversary Collections and Events

For some associate staff who have served in the same church for a number of years, having an anniversary celebration with a chance to collect letters or notes of appreciation from the congregation is a meaningful way to reflect on ministry accomplishments and to be encouraged to remember the joys of ministry. This may be an awkward thing for associate staff members to initiate. But if they have a committee they work with closely, someone in this group might be confided in and willing to pursue this on behalf of the staff member. I (Kevin) had served in a church for five years when the Christian education board held a surprise picnic in my honor, and it was a wonderful time of celebration. What a lift to one's spirits! Having a photo album of notes and pictures from that kind of event can be a wonderful reminder of God's grace in ministry.

> Our greatest joys come in long tenures where we have seen growth and we've been able to watch teenagers grow up, go off to college, marry, have their own baby, and been able to share with them all along the way. On our fifteenth anniversary, the church put together a compilation of notes from the people. We periodically go back and read those notes. They are a great source of joy.
>
> —AN ASSOCIATE PASTOR

As you think about the tangible reminders cited above, ask yourself what would be meaningful to you and help you savor the joys of your ministry.

Weathering the Stresses of Ministry

Learning to savor the joys of ministry is important in part because we will experience times when life and ministry become difficult. Instead of clear sailing, we find ourselves swamped by stormy waves of ministry or personal problems. For some associate staff members, these storms are so overwhelming that they end up looking for a new congregation to serve or a new vocation. Leaving may be necessary in some situations, and those who leave should not be judged for not "hanging in there." God works with each of us differently and is able to cause "all things to work together for good, for those who are called according to his purpose" (Rom. 8:28). We need to focus on our own ministry situations and how we can best weather the difficulties we will face with perseverance in following God's direction in ministry.

As my first church staff position was drawing to a close, I wasn't sure if I should stay in vocational ministry. Without the support of my wife, Patty, and the encouragement of other friends in ministry, it would have been all too easy to chuck it all and look for something different to do. I did explore the possibility of working as an editor for a curriculum publisher, but God opened other doors, confirmed my sense of calling, and encouraged me to continue on in an associate staff ministry at a new church. This was a very challenging time, and it was only by God's grace that I continued on in vocational ministry.

Like me, other long-term associate staff who are thriving in their ministries have not had all clear sailing. They too have experienced ministry and personal storms that could have taken them out of vocational ministry. In the midst of their difficulties, by God's grace, they found ways to weather the stresses and persevere until the tumult passed. Their reflections on how they weathered these times of discouragement reveal concrete steps that you may want to work through in your difficult situations.

Seeking God's Guidance and Help

The first response to ministry difficulties is to talk to and listen to God, humbly seeking divine guidance. It is an acknowledgment that full knowledge and wisdom reside in God, and that I may be ignorant, blind, and even wrong in things I have done or how I perceive the situation. My only hope for making it through this present difficulty resides in God's guidance and grace.

> I always go back and ask the Lord, "What am I to learn through this?" as opposed to "These are the problems and these are the people that are frustrating me." That's been good, because I

think we always need to be humbled. You know, we are not always right, and we are in a growing process. We haven't arrived.
—A CHILDREN'S PASTOR

A humble spirit before God is critical for learning and growing in ministry. I may have made mistakes, or I may lack the wisdom to deal with the current situation, but I serve a God in whom all wisdom resides (James 1:5–8). If I open myself up to God's instruction, through the means and people God provides, I can learn, grow, and become a better servant leader in the church.

The associate staff members who participated in these studies identified three particular practices that help them seek God's guidance and help in their times of need: taking mini-retreats, keeping a journal, and pursuing God in focused prayer.

Taking mini-retreats. For some people, getting time away on a mini-retreat is helpful. Having the opportunity to get away from the situation, even from the people involved, can help staff members gain new perspective. This time away with God can help heal emotional hurts and reduce defensiveness so that they can hear what God may want to teach them.

> There are times when I just have to be away from everyone, times when I am so wounded I need to be away from people. This gives me time and distance to heal.
> —A DISCIPLESHIP PASTOR

> Sometimes I have to take the afternoon off and say, "You know, I can't do any more. I'm not working any good for anybody. Lord, I need time with you. I'm going home or to the park."
> —A CHILDREN'S PASTOR

Keeping a journal. Some associate staff find that taking time to write their thoughts and concerns in the form of a journal or letter to God is beneficial. It helps them sort through their feelings, bring their needs and concerns directly to God, and open their hearts to hear what God may want to say to them.

> I journal. I share my frustrations with God, releasing the control back over to him. Usually by the time I shut the journal

> I feel like it's God's battle, and I'll let him change things that
> he needs to change, and even change my heart if he needs to
> change my heart. That's probably the biggest help for me with
> my frustrations.
>
> —A WOMEN'S MINISTRY STAFF MEMBER

Pursuing God in focused prayer. Our own sanctuaries can be places
of retreat for periods of prayer. Even though we know that God hears
us wherever we pray, praying in the sanctuary can sometimes help us
focus our thoughts. We are reminded of God's presence as we have
worshiped there so often in the past. Praying there also serves as a
reminder of those we serve, and our obligation to bring their needs to
God as well.

> There is a spot down there; I might as well have kneepads.
> There is a spot in front of the altar that's mine. My knees fit
> there very comfortably. And I do a lot of praying.
>
> —AN ASSOCIATE PASTOR

Revisiting Your Calling and God's Guidance

When ministry stresses hit hard, they often cause us to question our
ability to serve, even whether we should be in ministry. During these
times of challenge, it can be helpful to take time to revisit our experience of calling to vocational ministry and to recall how we have been
directed and provided for in the past. One long-term associate staff
member commented that he was able to weather ministry storms in
the present because he had already seen how God had helped him
weather them in the past. For new associate staff, our first big storms
can scare us into thinking that we can't survive them, that we need
to abandon ship. But our veteran associate staff colleagues are able
to put current problems into perspective because they have seen and
remember how God has worked before.

Taking time to remember God's grace and provision in the past
can give hope and confidence in the present. We still need to seek
God's direction for the present, but we need not be ruled by fear that
we will not be able to handle the demands we face. God is able to
strengthen and guide us if we are to persevere where we are. We need
to remember that the ministry is not ours but God's.

I was reading in the Gospel of John this morning, and the first verse I read was "Let not your hearts be troubled. If you believe in God, believe also in me." The last verse I read was, "Remember, greater is he that is in you than he that is in the world." I think when I get most frustrated, I have to remember whose job it is, and who the ministry really belongs to, and almost take myself out and then analyze the situation. And that helps give a little more perspective to it and brings it back to reality.

—A CHILDREN'S PASTOR

In addition, it can also be helpful to review some of the built-in benefits of pastoral service. Every year Mick reminds his new students that God's call is an amazing privilege. Besides the sense of "oughtness" that comes with one's experience of calling, there are those perks in ministry that provide a sense of fulfillment and joy through the many challenges of our work. They include experiencing the spiritual life cycle of believers, dealing with eternal things on a daily basis, being with people and bringing to them God's love, and receiving the love of the people as they minister to us. One associate encourages us with this comment:

Consider this season to be a great privilege in that the Lord has enabled you to participate in his kingdom work. Not everyone gets to have the gifts, training, capacity, and opportunity to serve in vocational ministry. And for those that do, they don't always get to do it long term. Circumstances might lead you to work in a different career in the future. So count your trials as a blessing, my friend!

Seeking Support from Others

While being alone with God is helpful for restoring perspective and gaining direction, God has also provided us with people who can support us through the ministry difficulties we face. Scripture instructs us to bear one another's burdens (Gal. 6:2), encourage one another and build each other up (1 Thess. 5:11), pray for one another (James 5:16), and stimulate one another to love and good deeds (Heb. 10:24). God knows that we gain great encouragement from the ministry of others in our lives, and it does not signal a lack of spiritual maturity to turn to others for support when we find our ministry demands overwhelming.

In chapter 6 we address the variety of supportive relationships that associate staff members can develop to help them thrive in ministry. When we face problems in ministry, these people listen to us as we talk through our feelings and concerns, offer wise counsel and personal support, hold us accountable for our actions, and encourage and pray for us. They are channels of the Holy Spirit in guiding and supporting us. The richest people in associate staff ministry are those who have both an open, intimate relationship with their Lord and Savior and the loving support of their brothers and sisters as they serve the family of God.

Adopting Practical Ways of Coping with Stress

Even while we seek God's counsel and direction in prayer, review our calling and God's provision in ministry, and seek the support of others as we face our ministry problems, we need to address the impact that ministry problems can have on us personally. Ministry storms dump a load of stress on us, taking a toll emotionally, physically, and spiritually. As we take action to reduce the causes of stress, we also need to cope with the stress we feel. (Chapter 7 has a fuller section dealing with ways of coping with stress in ministry.) As long-term associate staff reflected on ministry storms, they highlighted a few ways of dealing with the stress that accompanies them.

> If it's just stress because I'm not handling things well, sometimes I just need to voice it. I've got people that I can go to, to let off steam, leave it on their desk, and walk away. If it's stress because I don't have enough hours in the day, I know I can go to my supervisor and get help.
>
> —A CHILDREN'S PASTOR

> Having a hot tub helps a lot.
>
> —A CHILDREN'S PASTOR

> I go to the gym and work out, play my violin, listen to Scripture tapes and Scripture music.
>
> —A CHILDREN'S PASTOR

I have a couple of praise tapes that I put in, and I just praise God.

—A CHILDREN'S PASTOR

Sometimes just a good cry doesn't hurt at all.

—A CHILDREN'S PASTOR

You have to be real intentional about having fun! I've started taking country-western dance lessons this year. That's something I've wanted to do all my life. When things are getting stressful, I go out and dance, and it's a great mind relief. I just really, really enjoy that, and I can laugh, and play, and have fun. And then the next day I can come back and look at it again and have a fresh perspective.

—AN EDUCATIONAL MINISTRIES PASTOR

I have gotten to the point of writing names on golf balls and hitting them at the driving range. Taking two full weeks off each year really helps me. If I don't do that stuff, I flatline. I need to have times outside. Being single, sometimes I can't find someone to go with, however.

—ASSOCIATE PASTOR IN A LARGE CHURCH

I don't see my work as eight to five. I see it more in terms of seasons. Some seasons, like vacation Bible school or things like that, you just know they are going to have an all-out press to get everything done. But I try to reward myself after. I plan for a time that I can look forward to and say, this is going to be really hard work for this length of time, but after that, then I'm going to do these things with my family or for myself.

—A CHILDREN'S PASTOR

Finally, don't forget that God is able to relieve the stress we feel as we pray and receive the peace offered through the Holy Spirit. Paul admonished the Philippians: "Do not be anxious about anything, but in everything by prayer and supplication with thanksgiving let your requests be made known to God. And the peace of God, which surpasses all understanding, will guard your hearts and minds in Christ Jesus" (Phil. 4:6–7). God can be counted on to support and sustain us in all circumstances.

Taking Inventory: Questions for Reflection and Discussion

Whether you are just getting started or have been in associate staff ministry for many years, as you consider the ups and downs of ministry and how you are responding to your current ministry situation, it may be helpful to work through these questions, either on your own or with your spouse or a colleague. This can be an opportunity for you to encourage and support each other in savoring the joys and weathering the storms of ministry.

Savoring Joy in Ministry

1. When you think about your own joys in ministry, what things come to mind? Are you so focused on the stresses and problems of ministry that you are not seeing the ministry successes that could be an encouragement to you and increase your joy?
2. Do you have a "joy" file or box where you keep notes, pictures, and other mementos of your ministry? If you do, when is the last time you looked through it and took time to give thanks and praise for God's grace and goodness in your ministry? If not, start one now and look for things to put into it that can be reminders of ministry successes and joys. How could you use this file or box during times when you are struggling in ministry?
3. Do you have a picture board or some other way of displaying pictures and mementos of people and positive ministry experiences? If not, would having such a display be a helpful visual reminder of why God has called you to serve here and of the people who have been brought into your life and ministry?
4. Do you have a ministry anniversary milestone coming up that would be a good occasion to celebrate? How can you take initiative to do this, and to whom else could you turn who might help with the celebration? What would make it meaningful to you?

Weathering Ministry Stresses

1. When you face stresses and problems in your ministry, is your first reaction to grit your teeth and work harder, or are you taking time to pray for God's guidance, peace, and strength? How

much are you consciously turning to God for help in your ministry, and how much seems to be on your own effort?

2. Would taking time out for a mini-retreat help you gain perspective and strength for the ministry challenges you face? Can you get permission to do this? Are you getting adequate quiet time for prayer? If not, what needs to change to allow you this time?

3. When was the last time you reflected on how God has called, equipped, and guided you in ministry? Whom can you share your story with who can encourage you as you deal with ministry pressures? Perhaps writing your story out like a journal entry would be helpful in reviewing what God has done to strengthen and guide you.

4. What perks of ministry have you known—and are still there to encourage your heart? Have you been taking them for granted?

5. When you are under pressure in ministry, do you tend to isolate yourself, withdrawing from others who could encourage and help you? Who are the people you can turn to for support as you face ministry pressures and struggles? Do you need to take initiative in developing more supportive relationships, connecting with others, and supporting them in ministry as well? Read chapter 6 for more ideas on how you can strengthen this area of your life and ministry.

6. When ministry crises hit, how do you cope with the stress you feel? Do you have activities to relieve your stress? Are you using them? What else could you do that might help in managing the stress of ministry?

Part 2

Thriving Relationally

Introduction

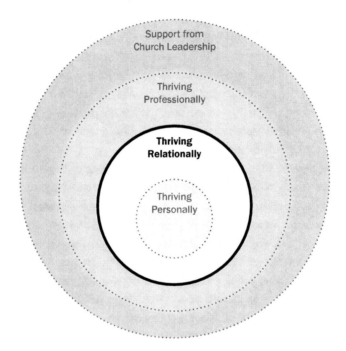

Support from
Church Leadership

Thriving
Professionally

**Thriving
Relationally**

Thriving
Personally

If pastoral ministry encompasses anything, it is human relationship. As asserted in part 1, a secure and growing personal relationship with Jesus Christ is at the very core of thriving, both personally and as an associate staff member. Being associates on faculty who help prepare men and women for ministerial service, we consistently emphasize that knowing one's field of service is necessary, but being able to live with and work alongside others is also critical.

In this section of the book, thriving associate staff describe features of their relational life that build, enhance, and support their positive experience in ministry settings. Considered by the vast majority of these respondents as of first importance, in chapter 4 we'll look at the home front, where the bonds of familial love affect the ongoing effectiveness and well-being of associate staff. Whether married or single, everyone is part of a nuclear family in which he or she can find various measures of nurture and encouragement while ministering within church or parachurch settings.

In chapter 5 we'll turn our attention to the working relationships thriving ministry staff enjoy with their supervisors and fellow associates. After family, most of our time is spent with these pastoral teammates. Our thriving associates will describe several key factors that create a positive work environment where staff can relish the joy of their calling. We'll uncover the personal characteristics that endear associate staff to their supervisors, helping foster a positive working relationship that can contribute to their ability to thrive in ministry together. And finally, these associates will reveal how specific attitudes toward one's fellow associate staff help create a rich working environment where everyone benefits.

Moving beyond the realms of family and work colleagues, chapter 6 will address the wide world of supportive relationships available in other arenas. Thriving associates report the fertile ground of friendships, prayer partners, peers and mentors, all of whom play unique supportive roles in their ministry leadership experiences. And as in all chapters, using a series of questions, you will be prompted to respond to these findings and ideas in light of your own staff experience.

Our journey into ministry began with our relationship with Jesus Christ. And being part of his church, we live, grow, and thrive in relationship with him and one another. May the ideas found here enable you to enjoy the bond shared with your family, work colleagues, and other special people God has given to you as means of grace and support.

4

Strengthening the Home Front

For if someone does not know how to manage his own household, how will he care for God's church? –1 TIMOTHY 3:5

One vital area of supportive relationships is the associate staff member's immediate family. In both the 1996–97 and the 2012 research, thriving associates overwhelmingly indicated the importance of family support. For associate staff who are married, no other relationship is as critical to the ability to thrive in ministry as the one with one's spouse. And, for associate staff who are parents, this role can bring with it added stress but also encouragement and joy. In addition, being the spouse or child of a church staff member can have its own unique stresses and frustrations, potentially undermining the family's relational health. If our relationships with our spouse and children are foundational to satisfaction in ministry, and if our ability to have a healthy family life faces potential threats, then it is important to find ways to reduce or prevent threats and to strengthen our family relationships.

This chapter begins with a look at the ways in which married associate staff members' relationships with their spouses and children help support them in their ministries. It then addresses the potential hazards of family life for an associate staff member and ways to strengthen family relationships. If you are single, we would encourage you to view this material as describing a template for building a healthy approach to marriage and family life in ministry. And at the end of the chapter, we'll hear wisdom from a few single associates who are experiencing satisfying and effective ministry.

The Power of a Supportive Spouse

Among married associate staff, no relationship is viewed as more important to the ability to thrive in ministry than the one with their spouse. More than 90 percent of the thriving associate staff members in our current study are married, and 97 percent of them identified their spouse's support as the single most powerful influence in their satisfaction and longevity in ministry.

Kevin and I (Mick) have both been blessed with wonderfully supportive spouses. My wife, Rolane, and I began serving together in church work when we were dating. Even then it was evident that all the time and effort we spent working out our future in ministry was worth it. We began to figure out how our spiritual gifts were complementary in our work with youth. As our personalities and views on ministry interacted, we began to develop our own unique team approach to pastoral service. After graduation I served as senior pastor, and my wife was very involved in ministry, in a congregation in the Pacific Northwest. Those eleven years gave us many opportunities to experience success, failure, blessing, and heartache. And we did it *together.*

Leaving this pastorate was a painful process. It involved leaving dear friends, a beautiful home and surrounding environment, and clear identities in our roles as pastor and pastor's wife. The move to Southern California with our twin nine-year-old daughters was an adventure. Finances were scant. Establishing new relationships and a new church home and figuring out the next chapter of ministry service drained our resources. But again, we did it *together.* By God's grace we navigated our way to what has become twenty-seven years of fulfilling work at the seminary where I teach and where Rolane is very involved in a support ministry to our graduates, and we are members of a most amazing fellowship of believers. Without the mutual commitment to Christ, one another, and pastoral ministry, our life story would read much differently.

Spouses can support associate staff members in a variety of ways. Long-term associate staff members who are thriving in their ministries describe seven aspects of spousal support.

Pursuing Calling

Many associate staff members were married before they considered pursuing vocational ministry. The decision to take on an associate staff position was one that had to be worked through together. Feeling supported by one's spouse in the decision to pursue God's calling to serve on a church staff is a wonderful experience. Knowing that your spouse sees you as someone God could use to serve others is powerful affirmation.

> My husband is my champion. There was a time when we grew apart rapidly . . . but when God called me back to ministry, we had a sit down and really talked about it. . . . He looked right at me and said, "You are made for ministry. If you don't do this, it will be the biggest mistake that we make as a couple. You have to do this." He got involved in a supportive role. He really was a part of supporting me in the ministry.
>
> —A CHURCH PLANTING ASSOCIATE PASTOR

Listening and Offering Perspective

One major way spouses assist and support associate staff members is by being a sounding board, listening to the joys and sorrows, frustrations and jubilations, problems and opportunities of their ministry experiences. Just having someone to listen and be concerned for you and your ministry helps.

> Next to coming to God himself, my wife is my sounding board. I can come home and tell her everything and anything, and she's always an encouragement. We pray together about it. She'll keep me focused on what I need to be doing to remedy the situation. She will offer suggestions, even though sometimes they are ones that I don't want to hear. I don't know how I could do the ministry without my wife.
>
> —A MINISTER OF CHRISTIAN EDUCATION

> When I come home totally discouraged over some thing or situation, he is always able to bring my perspective around. He has just been God's tool. He is able to bring my perspective back around to see it broader rather than this one situation that I think is going to kill me. You know, he helps me to see it so much broader. And his line is always, "The Lord called you into this. You didn't make a mistake. So let's you and I learn to work this thing out." That has been tremendous.
>
> —AN EDUCATIONAL MINISTRIES STAFF MEMBER

Encouraging

When associate staff members are discouraged, having a spouse who can offer words of encouragement can help them shake off the self-doubts and frustrations they carry. Sometimes we are so down that we've lost a proper perspective on who we are and what God is doing.

My wife and I have known firsthand how powerful an encouraging word is in pastoral work. Not only have we received countless notes, phone calls, and other expressions of support, we also have had the honor of being on the giving end. Through our support ministry to seminary alumni we seek to bolster the hearts and souls of our many graduates. What we hear back from them in appreciation is reflected in this associate's gratefulness for her spouse.

> My husband is my biggest cheerleader and would not let me quit. You know, when I come home and say I want to pack it in, he says, "No. You know those are your gifts, and that's where the Lord wants you to be." He believes in me when I don't even believe in myself.
>
> —A CHILDREN'S MINISTRY DIRECTOR

Promoting Personal Care

Spouses can be a support to associate staff members by helping them care for themselves and get the rest they need and by fostering an intimate, caring relationship. As couples grow to know each other over the years, they can help identify when the other needs time for rest or re-creation. Many associate staff members appreciate how their spouses help by caring for them and encouraging their spiritual growth.

> My wife and I have been married for six years, but before that we actually were in ministry together doing youth rallies and things. So she knows me so well that I don't have to tell her what happened. She can kind of read me and by the mood that I come home in she knows what to do. She can either go in the room and start praying for me or give me time just to sit and debrief or keep the kids away from me so I can think about things. She knows me and reads me like a book and helps me through it.
>
> —A YOUTH PASTOR

Praying

Many associate staff members look to their spouses as their number-one prayer supporter. Being able to share and pray with your spouse, having her or him bring your personal and ministry needs to God, is a strong source of encouragement.

> I'm one of those guys that believes with all of my heart that the role of a spouse is incredibly important. I could not do what I do if it weren't for her. I know she's praying for me. She's got my back, and I can tell that she's praying for me. When I come from a meeting the first thing she asks is, "How was the meeting? I was praying for you." If I have something intense going on during the day, I call her and ask her to pray for me . . . and I know she is.
>
> —AN ASSOCIATE PASTOR

Loving Critique

Sometimes a spouse is a support by being an honest, loving critic. Hearing criticism is not fun, but it can be a stimulus to improvement. When we know that the one who is critiquing our work loves us and has our best in mind, it is a little easier to accept the criticism. In the long run, we and our ministries benefit.

> My wife is one of my greatest critics, whether I want it or not. You know, a lot of times when I don't want it, it's probably when I need it most. She'll say, "What was that?" And it's good, because she looks at it through the perspective of just a person who isn't a musician, sitting out in the congregation. She is very honest with me.
>
> —A MUSIC MINISTER

Offering Hospitality

Sometimes an associate staff member's spouse is a support by allowing him or her to open their home and invite in people with whom they are ministering. This exercise of the gift of hospitality provides opportunities to enrich relationships and build a sense of being a team in ministry. Rolane has welcomed hundreds of seminary students into our home over the years. She cooks, bakes, cleans (with my help too), and decorates to make them feel welcome and part of the family. My feelings are reflected in this associate's observations.

> I couldn't do what I do without the help of my wife. She is supporting me, encouraging me, rooting for me, and then she is practically involved in a lot of things where she is strong and I'm weak. You know, she is excellent in planning the social events. The fellowship, the camaraderie, the fun that happens. And then the choir and the worship team come over on Saturday nights. So a lot of the relationships that have developed over the years have been because of her influence. And my children have all these aunts and uncles, you know, that have adopted them. We've got this sense of extended family because of my kids. It's a blessing.
>
> —A MINISTER OF MUSIC

The Ministry of Your Children

One striking finding of this study on what helps people thrive in associate staff ministry is the number of ways that their own children minister to them and make ministry more rewarding by their attitudes and actions. For associate staff with children, here is another opportunity to enjoy supportive relationships for ministry.

Our "first child" was identical twin girls. We didn't see them coming. Prenatal checkups never indicated two babies. In the first years of our Washington pastorate, life was busy enough, but when they came along the pressures grew exponentially. It was tempting at times to see them as an intrusion or competition with the demands of pastoral ministry. But as the years have passed and we now have midthirties, married daughters living for Jesus with their husbands and children, my wife and I see raising these delightful women as the best thing we have ever done together.

The Bible tells us that "children are a heritage from the LORD" (Ps. 127:3). For the minister, that is true in so many ways. Aside from the miracle of birth and the blessing children bring to the world at large, parents in pastoral service enjoy solid support from them in many forms. As thriving associate staff members reflected on ways that their children were an encouragement to them, they described four types of ministry received.

Unconditional Love

When my own kids were young and I returned home each day from working at the church, I often received a hero's welcome. It's funny, but when I showed up at the church office each day, people didn't run out to greet me, give me hugs and kisses, and tell me they were so glad I was there. But when I went home, I was warmly received by people who were just glad I was me and that I was home. Other associate staff share similar stories of the unconditional love they receive from their children and how it helps them weather the stresses of ministry.

> My family has been my joy and strength, like when the day has gone rotten and your youth meeting was the worst one you ever had. I have two little kids, and every time I walk through the door they go, "Daddy, Daddy, Daddy!" And they love me. And they don't expect me to entertain them or anything. They just want me to sit down and they want to climb in my lap.
>
> —A YOUTH PASTOR

Escape

Another way that our children minister to us is by providing another dimension to our lives. We are not just associate staff members; we are also parents. There may be frustrations, problems, and stresses in some aspect of our ministry responsibility, but at home, we are moms or dads. Switching from minister to parent can be stressful if the needs at home are great, but it can be refreshing if it allows us to escape the constancy of work pressures.

> I open my door and my kids run and say, "Dad, let's play basketball!" Learning how to forget your job is important. If I can forget my job when I close the door to my office and go home, I can be a dad now. I've got the next three hours to play with my kids and then I've got to go to another meeting. I love to play with my kids and just forget about it.
>
> —A CHILDREN'S PASTOR

In our ministry to alumni, my wife and I receive hundreds of newsletters from them each year. Those with children always include updates and pictures of their children, often times with more detail than they share about their ministry. It is evident to us that their children provide another world of reality apart from the pressures of the job, a world where they can play PTA parent, band booster, cheerleader, camp director, or just a lump on the floor to jump on (my fondest memories). Our children's world becomes ours, a place for intimate family sharing, jokes, and customs that are just for us, nobody else.

Help and Understanding

At times our children can provide practical assistance to us as we work to fulfill our ministry responsibilities. Even when our daughters were very young, they were extra helpful when we had houseguests, playing quietly in their room or entertaining other children, and generally keeping a good attitude throughout the evening. We thanked them for being a helpful part of our ministry to these families. As associate staff members see their own children's help and involvement in ministry, it is an encouragement to them to continue in their own ministry.

> Sometimes I've had to take curriculum home to prepare for teachers, which is quite an elaborate thing, and they have gone around the dinner table with me after dinner talking about things and sorted curriculum. I recently got remarried, and my daughter pretty literally took over the organization of preparation for VBS [vacation Bible school] and helped me sort things. When the kids were little, they used to come along and sleep in sleeping bags on the floor. It's been a big help to know that they've been very supportive of my work.
>
> —A CHILDREN'S PASTOR

> When I started, my children were younger, but now as they have gotten older, they have really gotten into children's ministries. All three of them are very capable in helping. My thirteen-year-old daughter could take a class and teach it as well as an adult, so it's been a good training time. But they've

also really picked up a real servant attitude. They will come into my office on Sunday morning after they've been to worship and Sunday school and say, "Mom, do you need help during the 11:00 service anywhere?" You know, they have the option of going home with their father, but it's just really given them a servant attitude, because they've seen it modeled. And that's joyful for my heart.

–A CHILDREN'S MINISTRY DIRECTOR

Personal Encouragement

When our own children express confidence in our calling to serve and a willingness to support us as we follow God's direction, that is a powerful source of encouragement. If we feel that our ministry decisions are hurting our children in any way, it becomes more stressful and difficult to determine how God is leading. Sometimes we can help our children understand more about the ministry God has called us to and seek their help in deciding how as a family we will deal with the new demands we face.

I have an eighteen-year-old and a fifteen-year-old, and their thoughts are not always the same as mine, but at least they are supportive. They can sense that this is what God wants me to do with my life. And so consequently, they are going to go with it. Even my fifteen-year-old right now, with all her relationships in high school, she believes that if God wants us to move, then we need to move and she would be willing to do that. She says, "Oh, I can make new friends somewhere else."

–AN ASSOCIATE PASTOR

With my kids, as they were growing up, the reason they were supportive is we used to sit down at our family council around the table, and they would decide how many nights Mom could have out. How many hours I could work at the church. Well, because we did that, then they were behind me in whatever I did. It wasn't, "Oh, yeah, Mom is gone again." And so when I would need a little help from them, it worked well.

–AN EDUCATIONAL MINISTRIES STAFF MEMBER

Threats to Healthy Family Life

Even under the most supportive circumstances, family life in pastoral ministry in any capacity is challenging. Rolane and I started our family life together in associate ministry. The pressures of being newly wed, finishing grad school, and working part-time jobs along with our church work served as a type of boot camp. And even though we were loved by many, the stresses of such a life presented a formidable test to our budding family life.

Years later, in a senior pastor role, we found ourselves again blessed with a wonderful local fellowship. But the threats to the health of our family were still very real, leading us to make crucial decisions along the way that protected and nurtured our relationships with one another and our daughters. While all vocations present challenges to one's family life, for people who serve on local church staff, several aspects of their unique calling can pose a threat. Here are some of the major areas of struggle.

Time and Schedule Demands

To some degree, associate staff members in a large congregation may have a better situation than most solo pastors. While solo pastors are on call twenty-four hours a day, associate staff members may find some relief from such an unrelenting schedule. Still, most staff positions carry heavy time demands, often resulting in part-time staff working full-time hours and full-time staff working fifty or more hours a week. In addition to the time demands, the fluctuating schedule of long evening meetings and weekend activities can make regular time with family difficult to maintain. Six to seven nights out at meetings each week for several weeks place a strain on relationships within the family. Spouses and children may end up feeling neglected, in competition with the associate staff member's work at the church. If this pattern continues, bitterness toward the church and ministry can result, along with damaged emotional ties within the family.

While we could mention this finding under any of the points here, 99 percent of the thriving associates we polled indicated that being able to "maintain a balance in my work and personal life" is one key to satisfaction and overall family health. Ministry is demanding work, requiring careful stewardship of time and energy for work and relationships.

Emotionally Draining Work

Along with heavy time demands and an erratic schedule, the very nature of some associate staff roles makes ministry an emotionally draining experience. Even work that we love can deplete us. Sometimes we live with the frustration of disappointing results. At other times, we find ourselves spent from difficult interactions with people we've been working with. On occasion we're just tired because we've been working long and hard. If associate staff members use up their emotional resources in their ministries and have scant reserves left when they go home, their families may suffer the consequences. Preoccupation, short tempers, emotional withdrawal, lack of energy for anything except watching television—all are ways we end up robbing our families of their spouse, father, or mother. If this pattern continues over time, it can further damage the quality of relationships within the family and the emotional well-being of all its members.

Unrealistic Congregational Expectations

Again, associate staff members in larger congregations may find that their experience is better than that of solo pastors. However, most associate staff members find that because of their church staff position, congregations place both spoken and unspoken expectations on their families. A married couple may feel the need to maintain the image of a perfect marriage, even when they are wrestling with serious problems. Their children may feel expected to act more mature than they are, to know the Bible better than other children, to be involved in every church program for kids their age, always to be well groomed and to "act nice." Spouses may feel pressure to have it all together and to take on ministry responsibilities outside the range of their gifts and interests. Both the associate staff member and the spouse may find it difficult to know how to handle and express negative emotions, especially in public settings.

Goldfish Bowl Experience

Related to congregational expectations and compounding the problem is the sense that the public is aware of one's family life. Because of their contacts with so many members of the congregation and their public roles in church leadership, many associate staff members feel as if they are under constant scrutiny. Everything they do, whether good or bad, easily becomes public knowledge within the congregation.

For example, when Rolane gave birth to our twins, they became instant celebrities. Literal crowds of people came to the hospital to see them together in their incubators. And picture this—when we brought them home to the parsonage located fifty feet from the church facility, they were put in isolation, meaning folks came up to our house to peer at them through the front picture window. This is true; you can't make this stuff up. We laugh about it now, but such is the life of leaders, especially in smaller towns and close-knit church families.

Awkwardness of Social Life

The high expectations they feel and the inability to escape the role of pastoral staff can make it difficult for some ministerial couples to have a normal social life. This may be less a problem in larger congregations and communities, but some associate staff find it difficult to make close friends they can be honest with, and not feel obliged to maintain a facade of perfection. Over time, this awkward situation can be discouraging to pastoral couples. Our interactions with hundreds of staff ministers over the years, including those in our most recent survey, have revealed this to be a major challenge. Those who thrive consistently report that they have been able to navigate these waters to find meaningful and trusting friendships, both within and outside their ministry contexts (see chapter 6).

In addition, being in a pastoral role typically removes the possibility of weekends away with friends or family. And there's the potential of not being able to afford the kind of social life many in your ministry can enjoy, making social events uncomfortable and often avoided altogether. Rolane and I served in a beautiful area near one of the nation's premier skiing venues. We skied once—with hand-me-down equipment and lift tickets provided by a loving family. It was fun but awkward. Many of you reading this can relate.

Lack of Self and Family Care

One issue that people in vocational ministry must deal with is the tendency to focus on serving and meeting the needs of others rather than paying enough attention to self-care. This orientation is common across the helping professions, contributing to a relatively high level of burnout. The danger for associate staff members is that they get so involved in ministry to others that they do not take adequate time for their own physical, emotional, and spiritual nurture. This same pattern can show up in a lack of proper care for their family members. It is like the shoemaker's children having no shoes. He is so busy making shoes for others that he never gets around to making them for his own children. Some associate staff can be so busy working with other people's children or other families that they end up neglecting their own.

Even today, as I worked on this chapter, a single student came into my office, plopped down, and confessed to being burned out and depressed. After an hour of conversation, it became clear this servant needed to focus on self-care. Too many good things were pulling this student and associate pastor into pieces. I'll be following up to make sure this lesson is well learned.

Impact of Technology

We are not about to assert that technology in and of itself is a threat to family life. But we do insist that it has an enormous impact on families, especially of ministry professionals. The six concerns above are all affected by the endless onslaught of advances in social media and other forms of connectivity. Keep this subject in mind as we address ways to improve and protect the health of your family unit.

Strengthening the Home Front

Every family has to learn to cope with the demands that parents' occupations place on family life. In spite of the struggles listed above, associate staff members and their families can find ways to foster healthy, supportive relationships together. Here are some specific ways that associate staff members can diminish threats to healthy family life and help themselves and their spouses and children thrive.

Protecting Time for Family

Although seasonal demands may take associate staff members away from their families for a time, staff members must find ways to keep this absence from becoming a pattern that interferes with strong family relationships. Here are some strategies that others have found helpful.

Ask for flexible scheduling. See if your church would allow you to take some time off during the day if you have a series of evening meetings that week. Take a break and come home when your kids get home from school if you have to go back after dinner for a meeting. Take time out from your day to attend your children's school and community activities. A lot of parents do not have the freedom to do so. It can be a nice perk of ministry. One thriving associate staff member offered this suggestion:

> Do *not* commit to a church that doesn't give you flexibility with your family time. Your family is dragged along to events, your spouse is often expected to serve, but if you're not given the flexibility to be able to go on a field trip with your kids or support your spouse without always having to take a vacation day, your church doesn't understand that long-term sustainability in ministry requires flexibility in your schedule.

Schedule date nights. Plan regular times out with your spouse and put them on the calendar. Don't let these dates get bumped off the schedule. If on occasion you have a conflict, reschedule; don't cancel. If money is tight, even an evening's walk and a cup of tea together is wonderful. It's not so much what you do that counts, but the fact that you do it together.

Schedule family nights. Same as date nights: Let your children help plan the dates and activities you will enjoy together, and don't let them get cancelled. On occasion, you may have to talk with your family about the need to reschedule a family night, but make sure it happens on the new date. Again, if money is tight, just making popcorn and playing a board game together can be fun. And don't forget the impact of spending time with your kids individually. That was especially important as my wife and I raised our twin daughters. They reveled in being recognized as individuals uniquely created and loved. If you are consistent in making this a priority, your children or spouse will not resent the occasional emergencies that get in the way.

Learning to delegate and delay. Strive to keep your schedule from getting overwhelmed. You may need to get your supervisor's help in determining what you really need to be doing, what can be done by others in the church, and what can wait until a future time when your schedule opens up. Also learn to delay nonessential meetings if they are interrupting scheduled family time. Kevin shared that he was playing a board game one Sunday afternoon when he received a call from a man in the congregation who wanted to discuss some theological issues related to a Sunday school class he was teaching. Kevin told him he'd be glad to talk later in the week; he was playing with his children right now. The man was a bit taken aback and offended that Kevin did not want to drop everything and discuss spiritual things with him. But the fact that the interruption was a spiritual matter did not mean it was more important than time with his children.

Pursue ministry together. If they are interested, try to find ways to include your children and spouse in some of your ministry responsibilities. This arrangement can provide you with time to talk and listen to your family members as you serve others together. My wife and I found ways to minister and have time with our kids simultaneously. Our church was located forty-five miles from major medical facilities. When someone was hospitalized, we would combine a trip to visit the sick with lunch at Pike Place Market. When appropriate, our girls were often allowed by the medical staff to join us in our patient visit. The possibilities are many!

Take time off and get away. Schedule your days off in advance and use them to get away from the concerns of ministry. You may find that you actually need to get away from your house, or from town, to put it all behind you and enjoy your time together. Resist the temptation to slip back for an evening meeting. Make it a real sabbath, a day of rest. Don't just do chores all day. Make sure you use all your yearly vacation allowance. I received three weeks per year, and we tried very hard to make sure two of those weeks were taken at one time. For most pastors, one week just does not cut it. We need several days in a row to decompress, enjoy the break, and then pressurize again for when we return to the office. One associate pastor explained, "When I'm on a vacation, when it's long enough, I want to get back to my ministry, which is a nice feeling."

Use technology to your advantage. There are a myriad of ways to harness the connectivity of today's technology. Creating a website for your ministry is just the start. Smartphone access and social network applications can be utilized to get information to people without taxing your personal time. And learn how to let the phone ring while engaged in family time. Most of us feel compelled to answer every call we receive. Why? Several of those we interviewed talked about training themselves to "let it go to voicemail" on their days off. They work hard at remembering that technology is best experienced as their servant, not master.

Have a daily meal together. Taking time each day to sit and talk with your family over a meal is a helpful way to stay connected with your children and spouse. If dinner doesn't work, breakfast might. Sometimes everyone in the family is so busy that it's almost impossible to pull this off, but it is worth the effort, even if it means coming home from work a little earlier than usual or getting up in the morning fifteen minutes earlier than normal. And remember, cell phones are put away while we eat!

Listen to your spouse and children. Pay attention to how your spouse and children are feeling about your work schedule. Listen to their comments, and take their feelings seriously. They need to know that they are important to you, even if you still have to go out tonight. Try to find ways to respond to their needs, such as scheduling special times together, getting permission to miss an upcoming meeting, or getting some time off during the day when you would normally be at the office.

> I definitely have to watch the amount of meetings and other things I take on, because I need to have more time with the kids and family, like helping with homework and other things. I definitely keep an eye on that. When the kids say, "Are you having another meeting tonight?" then I know maybe it's too much. I think the church basically understands. We try to make adjustments if we have a lot of evening meetings; then we take off some time during the day.
>
> —AN EDUCATIONAL MINISTRIES STAFF MEMBER

Managing Stress and Saving Energy for Your Family

Sometimes, even though we have time available to spend with our families, we're too tired, worn out, or stressed out to enjoy it. As a result, they don't enjoy it either. All we want to do is crash and have a nice long break from having to do anything with or for anybody. If you find that is happening to you, you may want to look at better ways to reduce or cope with the stress you face.

For associate staff members, along with the usual sources of stress in life, several aspects of work can become high-stress traps such as these:

- Ongoing volunteer recruitment difficulties
- Too heavy a workload for the position
- Insufficient salary and benefits to support a family
- Heavy work demands (especially seasonally, such as Easter, Christmas, summer camps, and so forth)
- Unresolved conflicts with the supervising pastor or other staff members (We will address these relationships in chapter 5.)
- Conflict within the church membership or particular ministry area supervised
- Lack of adequate supportive relationships
- Frequent interruptions from telephone callers and drop-in visitors
- Transitions within the ministry organization (for example, change of supervising pastor or other staff, budget cutbacks, reorganization of leadership, untimely departures of staff or members)

These and other sources of stress can tax one's ability to cope. The symptoms of too much stress can show up in different areas of our lives:

- *Physical* (loss of appetite, indigestion or heartburn, headaches, frequent illness, excessive fatigue, chest pain)
- *Psychological* (anxiety, depression, irritation, boredom, feelings of hopelessness or guilt, thoughts of running away or suicide)
- *Behavioral* (withdrawal from people, sleeping more or less than usual, difficulty concentrating, loss of interest in or distracting preoccupation with sex)
- *Spiritual* (feeling that God is distant, difficulty maintaining accustomed spiritual disciplines, withdrawal from fellowship or groups, feeling dry, "going through the motions" in worship or prayer)

If these symptoms are beginning to show up in your life, take them as a sign that you really are not doing well and that you need to make changes.

Three basic approaches can help you learn to cope with your stress holistically. We all employ some of these approaches some of the time, but when our stress loads go up, we have to learn to expand our coping styles and take better care of ourselves.[1]

Reducing Your Sources of Stress

Some of your stress may be self-imposed. Your self-expectations may be too high, driving you to tackle more than you should. Your interpretation of what is happening to you and why may be skewed, causing you to feel victimized or helpless to change anything. In these cases a change of perspective can help reduce the stress you feel. It may be helpful to seek out a good counselor who can help you reflect on your self-expectations and life perspective and adjust them to help you reduce your stress. Other practical steps that can reduce sources of stress include these:

- Setting goals and priorities to help you determine what to take on and what should wait for later or be handed off to someone else
- Addressing and resolving conflict situations instead of hiding from them and allowing them to fester
- Strengthening your time-management practices and scheduling skills
- Reducing overcommitments if possible through delegation, postponing, or getting help from others
- Seeking counsel from others who can help you deal with your problem areas

Coping with Unavoidable Stress

Since you cannot get rid of all the stress, develop good coping methods to help you face and work through it. Several helpful approaches include these:

- Keeping an open communication with God about your life situation through prayer and worship, seeking divine wisdom and strength
- Seeking out social support from a friend, talking through your issues with someone who cares for you
- Taking up enjoyable physical activities, reducing the effects of stress on your body, taking your mind off stress, and freeing up some endorphins (chemicals in the brain) to help you feel better
- Mental diversion through concerts, reading, movies
- Taking up a hobby or personal interest outside your work, such as gardening, crafts, or sports
- Taking mini-vacations or sabbaths away from your work

Building Your Health to Better Handle Stress

Finally, you can strengthen your capacity to handle stress through taking good care of yourself physically and spiritually. Adequate sleep, good nutrition, regular aerobic exercise, and spiritual disciplines that feed and strengthen you will help you cope better with the stress of life and ministry. Don't wait until you are stressed out. Take care of yourself, and seek God's strength in anticipation of the work demands you know will come.

Dealing with Congregational Expectations

As mentioned previously, you cannot totally escape the congregation's expectations of you and your family, but when those expectations are inappropriate or unhelpful, you can minimize their impact. For example, if you feel the pressure of having to display a perfect marriage and family at all times, you may need to develop friendships outside the congregation to give you the freedom to be more open about the ups and downs of family life and to escape the feeling that you are always being watched. If your spouse feels pressure to be involved in certain ministries in the church, he or she may need to take initiative early in your work in the congregation to identify his or her gifts for ministry and where they fit best, and then get involved in those areas. If your children feel they are expected always to be role models and on their best behavior, you may need to intervene on their behalf and help others understand that your children are no holier than others just because they are part of a staff member's family.

> A Sunday school teacher had to put my daughter in the corner because she was acting up. And that's good; I need her to be disciplined because she has ADHD [attention deficit hyperactivity disorder], and she needs to be dealt with at times. And the teacher kept going on and said, "We do expect more of our staff's children." And I went, "Wait a minute. I don't want you to expect one thing less from her, but don't you ever expect one thing more. She is a child, a human being. Don't do that." The lady was just stunned. My daughter doesn't get my paycheck at the end of the month, and she didn't necessarily get my calling. And I pray to God that she'll have the call to be a child of God, but not a youth minister's daughter. She never filled out the application for that.
>
> —A YOUTH PASTOR

Building a Rich Social Life Outside Your Congregation

Even though we may enjoy spending time with church staff and members and having time at home with our families, this limited range of friendships may not be enough for us or our spouses. The demands of work and family responsibilities may make it difficult to develop meaningful friendships with others. However, part of what helps people thrive in ministry is the range of supportive relationships they have developed and their ability to escape the stresses of life temporarily. While we will address such relationships in chapter 6, a few initial ideas for such support are appropriate here.

- Join a community sports league (softball, bowling, basketball, volleyball, curling) and get out to play once a week or more.
- Get tickets to a community theater or music ensemble and invite friends to go with you.
- Set aside two nights a month to invite a family over for dinner and board games.
- Go to local college or professional sports events with friends.

- Volunteer in a community-service organization, and invite others in the group to go out for coffee when your work is done.
- Recruit two other people or couples and take turns once a month hosting dinners in your homes.
- Throw seasonal parties, and look for excuses to celebrate life's special events with others.
- Get others to join you in skating, bowling, going to the beach, skiing, boating, fishing, walking, or some other favorite activity.

The important thing is to plan for these kinds of social gatherings and make them a regular part of your life. Just how frequently you do this, and how many people you want to spend time with, will depend on your and your spouse's personalities and interests.

Take Care in Sharing Frustrations at Home

Finally, while a spouse and children can offer great encouragement and support when we're feeling discouraged or frustrated with conditions at the church or in our ministries, we must be careful how we share our frustrations with them. Because they love us, they may quickly come to our defense and grow angry with others in the congregation. It can be helpful to unload frustrations on a good friend first, letting off some emotional steam that has built up. Then it may be appropriate to share with your spouse, discuss the frustration together, and pray together about it. Later, be sure to tell your spouse how the problem is resolved, and rejoice together when things go well.

> One reason why I don't share with my wife first is because she defends me to a fault. A half-hour conversation with her and I am convinced that they are all jerks. These other guys will tell me I'm a jerk sometimes. My wife, God bless her, she's so wonderful to me, she just defends me to a fault. I think that is a wonderful support, but you need the balance of perspective too.
>
> —A YOUTH PASTOR

Several associate staff also warned against talking about frustrations and conflicts with their children, cautioning that it can too easily sow seeds of resentment and bitterness toward the church.

Sometimes I have come home and caught myself griping and bringing up things that happened to me, and it started embittering my son and daughter against the church. "How dare they do that to you, Dad? You've done so much. I'm sick of this junk. They're a bunch of jerks. Why didn't you stay working for Pepsi, Dad? They treated you better." They don't need to hear any of this stuff. So maybe you should be honest, but I don't think that honesty does our children any good. I don't want to plant any seeds Satan can use for bitterness in my children. I want them to be in the church. I blew it, so I'm telling you from my mistakes. Be careful. Don't bring it to your kids; don't bring it up. I don't think it helps them.

—A YOUTH PASTOR

Balancing Personal and Family Care

One danger of a clear and strong call to ministry is that in our minds it can overshadow the other responsibilities God calls us to fulfill, including loving and caring for our family members and taking proper care of ourselves. We can become consumed with doing our ministry well and end up neglecting those closest to us. One long-term minister of music described his own struggles and insights:

I was probably a workaholic until my second child came along. The first child was pretty much left to my wife. I wasn't that interested in little babies anyway. The second child came along and was a child that didn't sleep, and my wife basically shut down. So I had to really rethink every aspect of life and ministry. I had some good mentors and role models on the staff at the church that helped me through that. Getting permission to do less around the church, even permission to do less than the congregation expected, not just less than I expected, was something I had to learn to do. That was a very good time, and I've been able to maintain some pretty healthy balance since then. When I see other music pastors getting into trouble because they're workaholics, it's just one more reminder that I don't have to do more than what God wants me to do. And one of the things God wants me to do is take care of my family. I'm the only dad my kids have. I'm the only husband my wife has.

Along with everything else said in this chapter, it is important that associate staff members who want to thrive in ministry over the long haul learn how to find an appropriate balance in their lives between the ministry and their care for their families and themselves. Many suggestions have been offered for taking time with your family and friends and for your own renewal. Make a commitment to spend time with your family on a regular basis and a commitment to your spouse and to God to nurture your own spiritual growth and emotional health. Let God give you a life that is full, not just busy. One respondent to our research mentioned a bit of wisdom he had received from one of his seminary professors: "Always protect your family time before ministry. I remember my prof's quote from years ago–'Your family is the first sheep among your flock.'"

Balancing family life and the work of ministry should not be a tug of war. We must view every relationship given to us by God as special, making sure to honor the priority of family commitments as we love and serve within the greater Christian community.

For the Single Associate Staff Member

At the outset of this chapter we recognized that many associate ministers are single, and we encouraged those of you who are to view these findings and recommendations as a resource for creating a template for any future married associate experience. We hope you have been able to benefit in this way. Yet, we realize that being single in ministry is both exemplified and encouraged in Scripture. Jesus himself never married, and Paul was single as he carried out his ministry. Paul encourages others who are able to remain single to do so, focusing their efforts on serving God (1 Cor. 7). Those who serve while single suffer no disadvantage in God's eyes and in fact may find it easier to follow God's call to ministry.

All associate staff members, whether married or single, benefit from developing supportive relationships with people outside their families. This need is evident in Paul's own letters as he greets and speaks fondly of those who have served with him and with whom he has shared fellowship. Single associate staff members may want to focus their efforts on nurturing a variety of supportive relationships that foster a family-like experience.

Sharing a house or apartment with friends, having supportive roommates to spend time with, talk with, and care for, can be an encouraging experience. If you live a distance from your parents, finding an older couple in your congregation or neighborhood with whom you can spend time and talk and who can serve as surrogate parents or grandparents can be of great support to you and may be a blessing to them as well. Finding a family in your church who will adopt you as a "cousin," "uncle," or "aunt" can result in rich relationships with them and their children as they grow. Forming close friendships with other singles in the church, enjoying activities, meals, and ministry together can be enriching to all concerned. Opportunities abound for loving, caring relationships to be built and close long-term friendships to be formed. Make the development of these kinds of supportive relationships a priority in your life and ministry.

> Both family and friends are important. Your family will support and encourage you for life no matter what is happening in the church where you serve. Yet local Christian friends are important, as well, as they may be more spiritually mature than certain family members. Having both a supportive family and encouraging friends gives great emotional support for the pastoral journey.
>
> —A SINGLE ASSOCIATE PASTOR

Taking Inventory: Questions for Reflection and Discussion

As you reflect on your family situation, the threats to healthy family life you face, and what you have already done to strengthen your family relationships, take some time to work through the questions that follow, either on your own or with someone else. Some questions to discuss with your spouse and your children are included. Take time to gain their perspective; it may give you new insight into what is needed and how to respond. If you are single, consider these questions in light of your relationships with close friends and extended family. In the larger scheme of things, marital status does not change the basic needs within all members of God's family.

Questions for You to Consider

1. Is your ongoing work schedule so demanding that you have little regular time with your family? Do you have time to spend talking with them, doing things together you all enjoy? If time is a problem, what options might your congregation consider to reduce the negative impact of your crowded schedule (for example, flexible scheduling, regular days off, delegation of responsibilities)?

2. Are your ministry demands so stressful or emotionally draining that the quality of the time you have with your family is affected? How are you coping with stress? From the stress-management section of this chapter, what could you begin doing that might help you better manage stress, freeing you to be a more enjoyable and supportive family member?

3. Do you feel (or do you think your family feels) pressure to have your family conform to some unrealistic, stressful congregational expectations? If you do, it may be helpful for you to discuss this issue with someone else, such as an older pastoral couple whom you respect, to sort through your feelings, discern how you are reading the congregation, and generate ways you might respond.

4. Are you feeling a lack of privacy as a family, as though you are always under scrutiny by others? Is this attention making it difficult for you to work through family problems or disagreements? If so, can you carve out times to get away from the congregation and community as a family and develop a greater sense of normal life?

5. Are you or your spouse feeling unable to make the close friendships and enjoy the kind of social life together that you would like? What opportunities are there in your congregation and community for you to get together with others with common interests? How can you make time in your schedule for such fellowship?

6. Do you feel that you have lost a sense of balance in fulfilling the roles and responsibilities God has given you in your family and work? What areas are suffering? What do you think is needed to restore that balance? What help do you need? How and where will you start?

Possible Questions for Discussion with Your Spouse

1. What do you like and not like about my being a church staff member? How do you think my ministry is affecting us and our family?
2. What kinds of stress or expectations do you feel because of my ministry responsibilities? How might I help you in reducing or coping with them?
3. Has my schedule over the past few months provided adequate time for us to spend together as a family? What do you wish we could do that we have not been able to do recently?
4. When I am at home, do I seem preoccupied or stressed out to the point that it interferes with relationships in our family?
5. How can I show my support and love for you better?

Possible Questions for Discussion with Your Children

1. What do you like and not like about my being a church staff member? How does what I do affect you?
2. How do you feel about the kind of work schedule I have to keep? What do you wish we could do that we have not been able to do recently?
3. Do you feel that my work makes me grumpy with you?

5

Working Well with Your Supervisor and Fellow Associates

Satisfaction in ministry proceeds from my relationship with the senior pastor. I think to the degree to which I am in tune with the senior pastor is one of the primary factors in whether ministry is satisfying to me or not. It is not as much for me the music making and the worship leading as much as it is that team that creates the satisfaction.

—A MINISTER OF MUSIC

My ministry life may not have started at all had it not been for a very special relationship with my senior pastor. As a second year seminarian, I (Mick) had come off an extremely difficult experience as a part-time youth pastor. The whole idea of serving in pastoral ministry had soured on me. After some weeks of confusion and negativity, "Sam" asked if I'd consider coming to serve with him as his associate. I hesitated, but he insisted I pray about it. What followed was over two years of fulfilling and joyful service alongside a man who remains one of my dearest friends. Upon graduation not only was I prepared for the pastorate but also I couldn't wait to embark on the journey. My friend's encouragement, mentoring, and team spirit helped revive in me a love for ministry that remains to this day.

Long-term associate staff members report that supportive work relationships with their supervisor (normally the senior pastor) and with other associates on staff (if any) are among the keys to thriving in ministry. Healthy and supportive staff relationships can make ministry seem like heaven, even when ministry demands and stresses are high. But relationships with a supervisor or fellow associates that deteriorate into mutual isolation, animosity, or indifference can take much of the joy out of even the best of ministry results.

As good as many staff situations are, none is perfect, and we all bring potential seeds of destruction into our work relationships in the form of our own sinful natures. Great work relationships with a ministry supervisor and other staff members do not just happen. They take commitment, effort, an awareness of those things that nurture or interfere with the health of those relationships, and the willingness to forgive. Building a thriving ministry environment is not so much about finding a great staff to join as it is learning how to make good work relations a high priority and contributing what you can to staff harmony.

Factors that Power Healthy Work Relationships

Ron had recently come on staff at his church as worship and music pastor. The choir had been working on a particularly difficult cantata and had just presented it that Sunday evening. To his trained ear, it sounded pretty good, but there were some rough spots that troubled him. When Ron arrived home later that night, the phone rang and he answered it. On the other end of the line he could hear the sound of people cheering and his pastor, rooting like an announcer at a baseball game, "It's the bottom of the ninth, the home team is behind, and the bases are loaded. Ron steps up to the plate, and there's the pitch. He swings and connects. It's going, going, gone! What a massive home run! We win!" Ron cheered too and cried, and on the wave of those words of encouragement, felt deep satisfaction in the role he had taken on.

On church staffs, as in most other work environments, much of people's satisfaction with their work is tied in some way to their relationship with their supervisor. One business professor Kevin spoke with went so far as to say that 80 percent of how people feel about their jobs is related directly or indirectly to their supervisors. For most local-church associate staff members, the supervisor is the senior pastor. Over two-thirds of the thriving associates polled in our most recent study were being supervised by their senior pastor; the rest by another staff member or executive pastor. Whoever the supervisor, that relationship can have a large influence on the environment in which the associate staff member works and can contribute to or detract from one's ability to thrive in ministry.

Recognizing that conflicts and frustrations can occur in many ways to undermine staff relationships and that building and maintaining good staff relationships take time and effort, let's look at some ways in which a positive working relationship with your supervisor can work to your benefit, turning a congregation setting into a place to thrive and to become more effective in ministry.

Trust

The most consistent comment made by thriving associate staff members is that their supervisor demonstrates trust in them and believes in their ministry abilities. Nearly every thriving associate staff in our newest study indicated that this was true of their work relationships with their supervisors, and they rated it highly in its impact on their sense of thriving. Indeed, such trust is a precious commodity, as implied by this biblical reference: "Many a man proclaims his own steadfast love, but a faithful man who can find?" (Prov. 20:6).

This trust allows them to exercise appropriate authority, make decisions, try new initiatives, and have a measure of flexibility in how they carry out their ministries. This trust is not automatic, and it cannot be demanded by the associate staff member. It is a quality that develops and is tested and confirmed over time. One minister of music described how his senior pastor's trust helped him thrive in ministry.

> Knowing that you as an associate have the authority to perform your ministry, to make decisions without having to get his thumbprint on everything [is important]. But that only comes with trust. And trust is not given; trust is earned. The way you gain that is, of course, by communicating that you are on the same page and where you are going in the ministry together, and [having] accountability.

Encouragement and Affirmation

Not everyone feels the same need for, or appreciation of, their supervisor's private or public encouragement or affirmation. Many associate staff (more than 95 percent in our study), however, report praise or affirmation from a supervisor a boost to their spirits and a motivator to continue pouring energy into ministry. This sentiment may be especially true for associates whose work is not as public as that of others and who therefore get less feedback from the congregation.

Associate ministers we conversed with indicated what such support meant for them. Their comments included things like these:

> It validates me in front of the whole church.

> It makes me feel legitimate, valued.

> It affirms the authority I have been given to minister here.

> It shows the congregation we are all on the team together.

Such encouragement can come only when there is a good working relationship between senior or supervising leaders and their staff.

Loyalty

Few actions by supervisors have more impact on your feelings about yourself and your ministry than the way they respond when you or your work is criticized or attacked. Having a good working relationship with your supervisors enables them to come to your defense or buffer you from criticism until you have a chance to present your perspective on what has happened. Supervisors who believe in you and are loyal to you in difficult situations reduce your anxiety as you work through the conflict. We have consistently found that thriving associates have supervisors who demonstrate their loyalty to staff. One children's pastor described how important this quality was for her.

> I've been in my job for fourteen years at the same church, and there are a number of things that have kept me there—not that it has always been easy sailing. But one is the support of our senior pastor, who really believes in me and encourages me. And without his support and total loyalty, I don't think I could have survived.

Like trust, loyalty develops over time. As you demonstrate that you are a trustworthy person who exercises good judgment, your supervisor's confidence in you grows and her willingness to stand up for you in difficult times increases.

Feedback and Evaluation

When you have a good work relationship with your supervisor, you have greater freedom to go to him for feedback on your work. You are more confident in seeking his evaluation because you trust his motives and can receive what he has to say as loving counsel. When your work relationships are not going well, you fear evaluations, not trusting the motives or agendas of your supervisor. If you recognize that you need honest feedback on your work and that you can become more effective in ministry, you must work to develop the kind of relationship that makes evaluation a growing experience. This point is critical if you are going to continue to grow in effectiveness. When we asked associates how they felt about this, they responded:

> You want to know what you're doing is expected. That's huge. Evaluation also helps you do your best in the area of ministry you're called to. You want to give it your best effort.

> In our environment we don't have annual reviews, but we are communicating so much that it's like a weekly review. We improve, change, and clarify our mission together. We have an ongoing conversation, a culture of review. It would be a drag for me to have to wait for an annual review, that's for sure.

Mentoring

Being mentored by a caring and qualified mentor is a great advantage in life. "Iron sharpens iron, and one man sharpens another" (Prov. 27:17). However, not all supervisors seek or feel they are trained to be strong mentors in the lives of their associates, but when staff relationships are good, some mentoring naturally takes place. When you gain trust and work well with your supervisors, you're in a better position to observe how they function in their ministries, to discuss ministry issues together, and to benefit from their counsel and experience. This experience is especially important for new staff members, but even veteran associate staff can benefit from a mentoring or mutual-mentoring experience. Chapter 6 includes more discussion on developing mentoring relationships.

Partnership

Another relationship aspect that thriving associate staff consistently rate highly is being treated as full ministry partners by their supervisors. They feel that they are part of the ministerial team, not just assistants or hirelings. While the basic ministry and leadership philosophy of the supervisor is a key factor in supporting a healthy team environment, this kind of partnership feeling can never develop when the work relationship between supervisor and associate is strained. Working well together enables the supervisor to view her associates as partners in ministry, and her voicing that perspective can boost your sense of commitment to and responsibility for the ministry. It can motivate you to do your best in your area of responsibility and to take an interest in the ministry responsibilities of others on staff. This mutual concern and support energize a staff and build relationships that encourage all in their work.

Shared Vision and Philosophy

Thriving associates serve in settings where they share creedal foundations with their supervisors and fellow staff colleagues. But equally significant to ministerial satisfaction and effectiveness is agreement among leaders on vision and philosophy. Ancient wisdom reflects such assertions: "Can two people walk together without agreeing on the direction?" (Amos 3:3, NLT). One respondent in our most recent research noted that "a team environment where common vision is shared concerning the purpose of the church and philosophy behind doing ministry" provides the optimal culture for thriving. Connected to hundreds of pastors over many years, both senior and associate, Kevin and I have noticed how the vast majority of problems arise on church staffs when there is significant discord regarding vision and philosophy. One should never underestimate their power.

Public Affirmation

A positive work relationship with a supervisor encourages the supervisor to lift up your ministry and give it credibility across the congregation. When the supervisor knows what you are doing, sees your hard work and good results, and shares this knowledge with others in the congregation, your reputation as a minister grows. This credibility opens the way for you to take new initiatives and introduce different ways of doing things, because the general trust level in your leadership is high. One associate blessed with a good sense of humor reflected, "A huge part of my very positive experience was having a senior pastor that fully trusted me and supported me in my gifts. I felt like a true partner in the fullest sense (well, except in pay!)."

Responding to Your Supervisor's Needs

During my years in pastoral ministry, I served in associate and supervisorial roles. And though others have said I can supervise fairly effectively, it is not my favorite task. My first few years in the pastorate were solo, and I supervised only volunteers. But soon I found myself overseeing paid staff, and that was a challenge. This was something new to me, and learning how to manage others brought on a whole new level of stress. But I have no doubt that as my associates and I developed the following workplace qualities, my supervising role became much more enjoyable. That is still the case in my present supervising roles at the seminary.

As an associate, when you recognize the benefits that can flow from a good working relationship with your supervisor, the logical question to ask yourself is, what can I do to help bring this about? On the one hand, I could recommend that as you interview for a staff position you look for a wonderful supervisor who exhibits all the qualities and practices addressed in chapter 10. That is probably too idealistic, however, and ignores an important aspect of how work relationships come about. A great working relationship between staff and supervisor is a two-way effort that develops over time and depends greatly on the attitudes, commitments, expectations, and grace that each person brings to it. Great work relationships are built over time, and each person is responsible for his or her own actions and attitudes, not the other person's.

If you take seriously the model of servant leadership portrayed in Jesus's life and teaching with his disciples (Mark 10:42–45), then your first concern as an associate staff member is to strive to understand what your supervisor needs and values from you and then to serve him by meeting those needs to the best of your ability. This approach opens the pathway for a positive work environment to develop and flow into your life and ministry. But what does your supervisor need and value from you? Our study identified several issues that are important to supervising pastors. We believe that if you will recognize what your supervisor needs from you and address these needs, you can contribute significantly to creating a positive work relationship that can benefit you both and the total ministry of the church as well. Here is what we learned:

Cooperation

Supervisors need to see a cooperative spirit in their staff or the task of supervision becomes an unpleasant chore and communication can shut down. A cooperative spirit is shown through words and actions that demonstrate respect, support, and a team spirit. Taking the initiative to ask if there is anything you can do to help, bringing your concerns to your supervisor with a teachable spirit, and listening attentively and drawing out her perspectives on issues you're dealing with all foster a spirit of cooperation. An associate's competitive spirit that seeks to strengthen his ministry agenda at the expense of other church leaders undermines the supervisor's ability to trust the staff member. Commitment to function as members of a diverse team, and not as competing kingdom builders, is critical.

Loyalty

The need for a sense of loyalty is felt by supervisors as well as by their associate staff members. Supervisors need to know that their staff will act in ways that demonstrate loyalty, even when there may be honest disagreement on ministry issues. Such disagreements need to remain matters for private discussion and not become public issues that can divide a congregation or undermine the supervisor's leadership. Talking behind the supervisor's back instead of dealing directly with him destroys his ability to trust you.

It is unfortunate that people who have complaints about a supervisor often seek a sympathetic ear in order to gain support for their grievances. They may come to you, praising your ministry and criticizing your supervisor's. Even if you privately agree, how you deflect the criticism and redirect the complainer to deal directly with your supervisor is important. There must be no appearance of division, but rather you must encourage people to deal with conflicts and disagreements appropriately. Your supervisor will value this kind of support. One of our recent respondents gave this advice: "Be ferociously loyal, never usurp, model followership, make the leader totally confident that he never needs to wonder about you, you are totally loyal, and always have his back–totally."

Honesty

Loyalty demands honesty. Supervisors need to know what staff members think and feel about their ministries, decisions discussed by the staff, and the ministry needs they see. Honest, open communication is critical for people to function well together on staff. A lack of honesty can cause people to put up defenses or shut down communication altogether. But honesty does not trump loyalty in all settings. Where disagreements remain between staff members and their supervisors, the staff should not discuss those differences in the congregation, even in the name of "honesty." Those discussions should be in private.

Of course, honesty is not something easily practiced, especially when we are not certain our supervisor will receive it well. Our delivery may not come across with grace, or she may not perceive of a situation as we do. The complexities of open interaction between flawed human beings are many. But far better to risk being misunderstood when speaking truth than to function in a relationship built upon falsehood.

Competence

Supervisors want to work with associates who have the basic competencies to carry out their ministry responsibilities. Some supervisors welcome the opportunity to help someone develop his skills further, while others want to be able to delegate a ministry area fully to their associate staff and not have to do any mentoring or staff development.

Especially if you are a new associate staff member, you need to know what level of competence your supervisor expects and to what degree he or she is willing to help you develop needed ministry skills over time. Ninety-five percent of the thriving associates in our survey cited supervisors who encourage them to keep learning and growing both personally and professionally. If you find that you need more assistance than your supervisor is able to give, you may need to find someone else with experience to whom you can turn for mentoring. But such an investment will pay high dividends.

Initiative

Competence without initiative may result in little being accomplished. Again, supervisors differ in how much initiative they expect their associates to take and how much they themselves want to give direction to and momentum with which the ministry is carried out. Most supervisors expect their associates to take some initiative in their work and not need to be told what to do all the time. This expectation is related to the level of competence the supervisor expects in her associates and the degree of responsibility and authority she is willing to delegate. How much is delegated may change over time as you gain ministry experience and demonstrate a growing level of competence.

This seems a good place to address how to avoid contributing to a situation where you may experience micromanagement. The thriving associates we hear from are virtually unanimous in their praise for supervisors who *don't* do this. They advise being a self-starter, motivated from within to pursue your ministry with energy and initiative. This gives the senior staff person the sense of confidence she needs to let you fulfill your responsibilities without the burden of having to scrutinize every move you make.

Trustworthiness

Just as associate staff members want to feel that their supervisors trust them in their ministry, supervisors want to feel that their associates are completely trustworthy. This quality relates to loyalty and to other issues as well. Supervisors need to know that if they delegate a responsibility to an associate and the associate receives that responsibility and agrees to see it through, it will indeed be done. They want to know that matters shared confidentially in staff meetings will remain within the staff and not be mentioned outside. They need to feel that their associate staff can be trusted with the resources of the congregation and the lives of the people in their care.

Trust is established and tested over time but remains fragile. It is easily broken by careless words and actions. Associates must be conscious of the trust that has been extended to them and honor it by faithful action. If you violate your supervisor's trust in you, Christ calls on you to ask forgiveness and to be reconciled with your supervisor. While forgiveness may be extended, time is required for the damage done to the work relationship to be repaired and for reconciliation to be complete. While restoring working relationships might seem an impossible task in the secular business community, within the body of Christ we have Christ as our example of one who extends grace and who reconciles us to God and to each other.

Open Communication

One youth pastor described the attitude of many supervisors when he quoted his own supervisor's words to him about communication: "All I ask is that you keep me informed. I don't like surprises." Supervisors need to know what's happening in their associate's ministry areas, especially new program initiatives and anything that affects other ministry areas. They don't want to be caught unaware of what their associate is doing. Supervisors vary in the level of detail that they want to be given, so it is better to discuss this preference with your supervisor ahead of time. In general, err on the side of too much information rather than too little. Comments from those we surveyed underscore this advice.

> Overcommunicate with your senior pastor. This allows for more trust and freedom to exercise your gifts and move your ministry in the direction you want.

> Overcommunicate—there is a tendency to not know the big idea and who's in charge of what. Ask, ask again, and then re-ask.

Supervisors should also understand your needs so that they can determine how best to respond to them. You need to speak openly about what will help you be more effective in your work.

While all the needs listed here are important to developing good staff relationships with a supervisor, some supervisors will be more sensitive to some areas than others, due to past experience or present circumstances. It's important to discuss these needs together so that you can best understand how to serve your supervisor and flourish in your ministry area as well.

Working with Fellow Associates

While your relationship with your supervisor is a critical factor for thriving in ministry, your work relationships with other associate staff members are also important. Whether you work closely together on common tasks or each have your own separate area of responsibility, you have the opportunity to create a supportive work environment where each associate can benefit from the interest, wisdom, and assistance of others in the group. Being part of a larger ministry team provides a sense of belonging, security, and support and can be an important factor in your thriving in ministry. (In many cases, this larger ministry team may include key lay leaders as well as other associate staff members.) This kind of relationship does not come about automatically. Too often associate staff members treat each other as competitors instead of seeing each other as teammates. Creating a team environment is the result of consistently living out several important team commitments.

Cooperation, Not Competition

Kevin shared a story from his ministry experience on staff that was painful to remember.

> I had just begun working at my second church and needed to arrange to use one of the church's buses for a youth event. I checked our reservation calendar and discovered that the minister of music had the large bus reserved for the same date I needed it. Not only that, but he had reserved one or both buses for several other dates over the next few months for choir trips.

> Suddenly, rather than seeing him as an ally in ministry, I be-
> gan to see him as a competitor for scarce resources. Rather
> than talking with him about working out schedule conflicts,
> I began to plan my activities far ahead so I could be sure to
> reserve the buses before he did. It's amazing how selfish and
> stupid I could become over a bus.

The first and major overarching commitment in working with
other associates is to develop a spirit and mindset of cooperation and
partnership, not competition. A competitive spirit focuses on *my* ministry, while a cooperative spirit focuses on *our* ministry. A competitive
spirit is unsettling to all involved, creating a climate of suspicion and
making fellowship in ministry difficult to attain. A cooperative spirit
and the harmony that develops as you work together encourage longevity and satisfaction in ministry. One children's ministry director
described the impact of harmony on her work relationships with fellow staff members.

> If there is harmony on staff, then that can really extend the
> longevity so we don't want to leave. Because if we left, we
> would just go off and start a used-car lot, sales business, or
> something together. Sticking together is very important for us
> because we feel that God has brought us together.

Mutual Concern

Commit yourself to being concerned with the ministries of others on
staff and with their personal well-being. Discipline is required here,
because your heart and energies can be so wrapped up in your own
area of ministry. It requires a cooperative spirit and the growth of a
vision of the church's ministry larger than your own area of responsibility. It also requires a willingness to open your life and ministry to
the interest and concern of others. When you recognize that you are
on the same team, your interest in and concern for the ministries of
others are able to grow. A director of Christian education describes
how this attitude has affected his own longevity in ministry.

> A big thing that has kept me [here] is the sense that we're all
> in it together, really interested in each other's ministries. I'm

free to absolutely lead without [others] asking questions in my area, but there is such support there. And I'm just as interested in the youth ministry and in the adult ministry. We're just all building up each other's ministry.

This aim has not always been easy for either Kevin or me to live out. When the pressure in our own ministry areas or personal lives is great, we can too easily focus inward and lose sight of our roles as part of larger teams. Kevin relates:

I was lovingly confronted one day at a staff meeting when I had finished my agenda items and the associate pastor began to raise some issues in his ministry area. I asked to be excused to get back to work on something, and he pointed out that he had patiently sat and listened to me discuss my ministry needs many times and that he valued my perspective and input as he wrestled with his. His words brought me up short and gave me a renewed understanding of what it meant to be partners together on a ministry team.

The two of us have served as fellow faculty (associates) in our university context for many years. We have been privileged to witness and personally receive prayerful and purposeful concern from our colleagues through many challenging circumstances, both public and private. I always share with students my prayer for them that they will know the kind of staff environment we have enjoyed consistently over these years. Which leads to our third point.

Mutual Encouragement

As you recognize that you are teammates and your concern for others' ministries and personal well-being grows, encouraging and lifting each other up in times of difficulty becomes more natural. Encouraging each other when the ministry is not going well and listening to each other's personal struggles are important elements in building up our teammates in ministry. A youth pastor explained how this kind of encouragement affected him in ministry.

We're all supportive of one another. When we meet together, if something happens, if somebody dropped the ball, we don't point the finger and say, "You blew it." We all carry it together. It's such a team and such a family, which is incredible. You don't kick the son or the daughter out of the house because they blew it one time. We're there, supportive of one another, encouraging one another. "How can we get through this together?" I think that's a sign of a healthy organization, a healthy church, and that's nice to be a part of something like that. I'm privileged to be a part of a great church that's like that.

A women's ministry staff member described the personal impact of the concern other staff had for her, not only for her ministry area:

We have a large staff. There are about twenty-two of us. So when we get together, we sometimes give the instruction when we are ready to pray, "Let this be personal. Let's don't get off on our ministries." When we are worshiping, we'll say, "Keep the ministry things out of this. Let's come and let's be personal with this." So we have a time for that in our staff meeting. I feel like every one of those men are my brothers. When I came along, there were twelve of us. I felt like I gained eleven brothers. You can't be close to all eleven of them all the same. So I have a couple of them that if I am hurting with something, I'll go to their office, or they'll go by my door and I'll invite them in. Then I can stop and pray with or just talk with them, be really bottom-line with them [about] where I'm hurting.

Mutual Aid

A natural result of mutual concern and encouragement is the offering of aid to each other when there are ministry needs. While each staff member is to carry his or her own workload, at times we need the assistance of others to handle a sudden increase in ministry demands. The willingness to help grows out of a teammate vision of ministry, an awareness of each other's needs, and a commitment to each other's success in ministry. Two associates serving in midsized congregations noted:

One of the things I do, and I'm in a position to do it, is offer my help in other areas—especially if they have a project, like VBS. I'll go to the director of children's ministries and say, "How can I help?" Later today I'm going to help another staff totally rearrange the sanctuary. I think that kind of help is important. It keeps us all together, builds relationships, the kind that aren't a product of "staff meetings."

Showing up for stuff not in your area is huge. You don't need to supervise it; you're not there to teach. Being there to support the ministry, not to be critical, helps build trust and shows that you care. We tend to get "siloed" into our own area, but we can take an hour here or there.

A youth pastor described how mutual assistance and concern helped sustain him through some difficult times in ministry. In his case, the concern and help came primarily from lay leaders closely involved with the work of the church staff:

But when you do have the staff or the church board behind you supporting you. . . . Like at the church I'm at now, the chairman of the church said, "I've got your back covered. I'm going to be there supporting you and going to bat for you anytime you need it. And I'm going to be praying for you." And I have people from the church constantly calling me saying that they're praying for me and encouraging me in the youth ministry. We just had a youth closely related to our youth group commit suicide. And then right after that, we had a girl that was in a severe car wreck, and her face was mangled and we didn't think that she was going to live. And these things happened back to back, and it was just a horrid time for us. And it's those times that the church members are calling me saying, "Mike, I'm praying for you. I know you've got a tough job ahead of you with the funeral and with the other girl." And the chairman of the board said the same thing: "If you need me to cover for you for anything, I've got it." And so that really helps.

The willingness to invest time and energy to help your teammates builds a climate that makes ministry together a joy. When ministry successes come, they are *our* cause to praise God, not just yours.

Mutual Mentoring

Several years ago, after moving from a senior pastor position to my present faculty ministry, I was chatting with one of our distinguished senior theology faculty. He turned to me and asked me a question related to the practical outworking of a church leadership polity prescribed in Scripture. I was stunned he would ask me, a rookie teacher and many years his junior. Not only was my sense of significance bolstered, but I also learned a lot about how impactful mentoring can be, whether as mentor or protégé.

Mutual mentoring among associate staff members is one of the great blessings of serving with others on staff. As you minister with others and strive for supportive work relationships together, you will have many opportunities to learn from them and possibly teach them as well. When you make this a commitment together, you seek ways to learn from each other the skills, attitudes, and information that will make each of you more effective.

Mutual Fun and Socializing

Thriving pastors report that they enjoy socializing together (89 percent). Seventy-one percent report their church staff has regular retreats together. Being on a ministry team with others does not automatically mean everyone will be the best of friends. Personalities, preferences, and life and family circumstances often preclude the kind of relationships we might envision. One children's director noted that she—as a wife, mother, full-time minister, and co-laborer with her husband in their agricultural business—simply "doesn't have the time" to deepen friendships with the other staff. Another youth pastor mentioned that she, being the only woman on staff and being much younger than them, does not feel comfortable socializing much with other staff. While such limitations are common to many staffs, the effort is worth it, as these associates report.

> It's easier to be confronted regarding a ministry issue if there's an actual relationship there. You get really close after some years, especially if you spend time together off the job. The socializing makes the job more personal, more fun, and more joyful.

> We're reading a book together as a staff, and one of the ideas
> the author expresses is that informal time leads to trust. And
> the trust allows us to have conflict. And we need to be able to
> address conflict as a team—that is so important.

Team ministry can and should be a place where spiritual vitality
and virtue are modeled and enjoyed by all. This does not come easily,
but thriving associates are blessed with this kind of environment and
are willing to invest to see it happen.

Taking Inventory Questions for Reflection and Discussion

Having reviewed these key conditions that serve the needs of senior
pastors and supervisors and those that foster better work relationships
with fellow associate staff members, here are some questions to help
you assess your current situation and explore ways you can contribute
to a more positive work experience for everyone.

A Few Questions If You Are Looking for an Associate Staff Position

While every work relationship develops over time, considering what
you really need from your potential supervisor to serve well and to
grow in your ministry responsibilities may be helpful. The better you
understand yourself and your potential supervisor, the easier it will
be to identify an appropriate fit for ministry. Here are some factors to
consider:

1. Some personality instruments, such as Myers-Briggs, DISC, Personal Style Inventory, and 16 Personality Factors can help you
   identify how you tend to interact with others in a work setting.
   Some congregations use one of these, or a similar instrument,
   in the interview process. Even if they don't, you might benefit
   from using one yourself so that you can be more aware of your
   strengths, limitations, and tendencies. Check with a seminary
   or denominational ministry placement center to see what its ex-
   perts recommend.
2. What is important to you as you consider joining a church staff?
   What questions can you ask that will help you better understand

not only the position but also the work relationships at the church, the expectations of the supervising pastor, and what the priorities are for the role you are considering? Don't be passive in the interview process but actively and tactfully try to learn what is important to the supervisor and what he or she is looking for in a candidate for this ministry position. A job description generally does not address this type of issue well enough.

3. Read and reflect on the questions below, not as a present reality but as a look at future ministry. What areas do you think could be stumbling blocks for you? To whom can you turn to talk through the areas you are not sure about?

Questions to Consider about Yourself

Think through your responses to these questions and their implications for working with your supervisor:

1. Do I serve in my ministry position with a cooperative spirit and a broad perspective on the church's ministry, not just focusing on the needs of my own ministry area?
2. Do I demonstrate loyalty to my supervisor, and if there are areas of disagreement, do I work to resolve them in private?
3. Am I open and honest in talking with my supervisor, not trying to push him or her to respond but encouraging better understanding and seeking to assist in resolving hurts, conflicts, or disagreements?
4. Do I work hard in my ministry, striving to grow in ministry skills and competence and to take on the level of initiative I have accepted from my supervisor?
5. Am I a person of integrity in my work, trustworthy with the resources and people I have responsibility for? If I need help in fulfilling my responsibilities, do I seek it?
6. How do I feel about being accountable to someone else for my ministry? Is there anything in my attitude toward authority or accountability that I need God's help to resolve?
7. What things am I hoping my supervisor will be able to do to help me grow in my ministry? Have I found a way to communicate these things to him or her?

8. Do I regularly pray for my supervisor that God would strengthen and guide him or her in ministry?

Questions to Discuss with Your Supervisor

Here are some questions that could be profitable to discuss with your supervisor. Strive to listen carefully, ask good follow-up questions, and see what you can learn about working well with your supervisor.

1. What three to five things could I do that would help you most as my supervisor?
2. What level of initiative do you want me to take as an associate in ministry, and in what kinds of situations do you want me to check with you first before taking action?
3. If you and I have disagreements about ministry issues, how would you like me to bring these to you and work them through with you?
4. What things could we do that would help in building a cooperative ministry together?
5. What three to five things do we need to discuss together to help me serve well and grow in ministry competence?
6. Are there any areas where one or the other of us has felt that trust or loyalty in our work relationship has been compromised? Has anything taken place that has caused our respect for each other to suffer? If so, what can we do to resolve the situation?

Questions to Think about or to Discuss with Fellow Associate Staff Members

If you serve with other associate staff members at your congregation, whether paid or volunteer, here are some items to think about or to discuss with them that could strengthen your working well as a ministry team.

1. What signs do I see that we are serving together with a cooperative spirit? What signs of unhealthy competition do I see? What's my role in moving toward a more cooperative spirit in ministry?

2. Are my eyes so much on my own ministry responsibilities that I have not expressed interest in and concern for the ministries of my colleagues? Do we function together as impersonal strangers, or are we expressing appropriate concern for each other as well as our ministries? If growth in this area is desired, what can I do that would be appreciated by my colleagues?

3. When was the last time I encouraged one of my colleagues in his or her ministry? Am I freely sharing with colleagues the good things I hear about their ministries? What am I doing to build them up?

4. Though all of us have our own ministry responsibilities, are there any areas where I could really use the assistance of one or more of my colleagues because of their gifts, abilities, or experience? Have I been afraid to ask for help for fear it will reflect badly on me?

5. What have I learned from my colleagues in ministry (about ministry, spiritual growth, taking care of my family)? Have I told them what I have learned from them and thanked them?

6. What areas need to be strengthened in our service together as staff? Where can we begin?

7. Do I regularly pray for my fellow associate staff that God would guide their ministries and meet their personal needs?

6

Building Supportive Relationships

Two are better than one, because they have a good reward for their toil. For if they fall, one will lift up his fellow. But woe to him who is alone when he falls and has not another to lift him up!
—ECCLESIASTES 4:9–10

One of the strongest and clearest messages from this research is that the ability to thrive in associate staff ministry is greatly strengthened by our relationships with others who support, encourage, challenge, comfort, pray for, and believe in us. We do not thrive well on our own, but we can in the company of others who care for us and come alongside us in various ways. If we are going to have longevity and satisfaction in ministry, we must intentionally build supportive relationships that will help us through the challenges of ministry. The associate staff member who functions in isolation and does not have others to turn to for support is in for a very rough ride.

In all my years of ministry, 75 percent of which have been in associate staff positions, I (Mick) continue to experience faithful and caring support from many wonderful people. Aside from my immediate family there have been seminary friends, pastoral staff colleagues, community leaders, members of local churches, and fellow faculty where I currently serve. In addition, I enjoy the ongoing support of several former students now serving in ministries worldwide. These and many more are God's gift to me as the years of service come and go. They are stewards of the grace of God, allowing me the amazing privilege of a fulfilled and thriving life of ministry (1 Pet. 4:10).

As thriving associate staff reflected on the supportive people God had used in their lives and ministries, several types of support were identified. As someone seeking to thrive in associate staff ministry over the years to come, you will find it helpful to consider the people God has already brought into your life who strengthen you for ministry and what further steps you may want to take to initiate and strengthen these kinds of supportive relationships.

Veteran associate staff describe six types of supportive relationships that have helped them thrive in ministry. In what follows, several associate staff reveal the nature of these relationships, how they came about, and why they have been so beneficial.

Friendships within the Congregation

There is an old warning in vocational ministry about not getting too close to the members of the congregation you serve for fear of causing cliques to form or jealousies to arise in the church. This concern has led some church staff members to remain distant from the laypeople they work with. Counter to this warning, a resounding 99 percent of the thriving associate staff who participated in our most recent study reported that their friendships with members of their congregations were a strong source of support that helped them thrive in ministry. Perhaps in a multiple-staff church setting the formation of supportive friendships with congregation members by associate staff is not as threatening to the unity or stability of the congregation as it is if the congregation has only one pastor.

Congregation members can be a tremendous source of encouragement and support for associate staff members. Some of these relationships develop because of the volunteer positions that bring them together to work on a common ministry. Others develop on a more informal level, not because they work together. The support comes in many forms, depending on the kind of relationship that has developed. Friends within the congregation can offer encouragement, sympathy, prayer support, new perspectives, and even loving confrontation. Here are some stories and descriptions of how these relationships have developed and how they helped support thriving associate staff members.

> I moved into a youth ministry department and had three very frustrating years. There were four men on the youth committee, and they became my covenant group. Each one of them

had a different task, and if it hadn't been for those four men I never would have survived. One called and told me the joke of the day, the chairman would take me out to lunch every once in a while, and another one would just give support. I think a support group like that is so important.

—A YOUTH PASTOR

I'm single, so I don't have a spouse or family. I don't live close to my family. For me, the support is friends. There is a couple in the church who are friends of mine. They aren't old enough to be my grandparents, but I call them Pops and Grandma. I can go over to their house and just kick back on the couch. They are sensitive enough to realize that I just need some space.

—A CHILDREN'S PASTOR

Even though I'm training, mentoring, and helping to develop our lay leaders, they very often have turned around and become my number-one support in praying for me, in caring about my needs, and just upholding me. And that has been a real surprise and a blessing as those people have become real special friends. I think that's one thing that really separates church ministry from a lot of other kinds of work . . . the friendships that you can have with the people who are serving with you.

—AN EDUCATIONAL MINISTRY STAFF MEMBER

I found a great deal of encouragement in a small accountability group in my church that was with nonmusical folks, not people that were involved in my ministry. Because of that we could talk about church, but we didn't talk about the details of music and worship ministry. We could talk more about personal things, because they are people that I didn't work with closely, week in and week out, just people that I developed friendships with. That was a real strong source of encouragement for me. It took a number of years to find and create that group.

—A MUSIC MINISTER

Friendships outside the Congregation

While friends within the congregation can be a great source of support in ministry, there are times when having friends outside the congregation can be helpful as well. Our 2012 study saw a significant rise in those reporting such friendships as a factor in their thriving (from 73 percent in 1998 to 90 percent in 2012). When you are experiencing difficulties or frustrations in your ministry, you may not always feel that it is wise to share these with others in the church. If they are close friends, they may try to defend you, carrying your frustration on their shoulders and becoming soured on others in the church. Many associate staff members find that at times they need to dump their frustrations on a friend who is not involved in their church. In some cases, just venting their frustrations helps them gain perspective and strength to go back and work through the issues. In other cases, the person they dump on can ask probing questions and help them identify constructive ways of responding to the situation. Those who are dumped on can often help associate staff members gain new perspective on the problem, even helping them see their own mistakes or faults and how they might resolve the current situation. One children's pastor described how important this kind of friendship is for her.

> I dump on my closest and dearest friends. We dump and take turns dumping. I try to talk it through with somebody outside the church that can give me a different perspective. I tend to go to my friends who I feel are very mature spiritually. They give me a godly perspective, godly and biblical counsel because of their background and training. And they don't just say, "Oh, poor Sally, she's just suffering so much." Yes, they're going to say that, but they also say, "All right, you idiot, why did you do thus and so?" They're going to confront me as well as comfort me. That's the kind of person I go to.

Friends from outside the congregation can also be a support to associate staff by providing them the opportunity to escape from ministry problems and spend time with others enjoying nonchurch activities and conversations. Just taking a break from discussing church concerns can be refreshing. One senior pastor with whom I worked enjoyed going duck hunting with community friends who did not attend our church. It was a mini-vacation from the stresses of ministry. A director of Christian education told of the benefits of spending time with people outside the church.

> We have some friends who are not part of our congregation. Most of our relationships, of course, are with people from the church. In ministry, basically your whole life revolves around the church. Even if you go out socially, generally the subject gets around to the church. We have scheduled times when we can get away with this other couple. I can spout off to them all I want. I can talk about people, and they don't know who they are. And he can do the same thing, because he is in Christian work. We don't know who he is talking about, and he doesn't know who we are talking about. We can just spill it all. That's been a help.

Prayer Partners

High on the list of supportive relationships are the individuals or small groups that associate staff members turn to for prayer support. Having someone to dump on is nice, but if that is where it stops, it falls short of the encouragement and support that God has called us to give to each other. Having people to whom you can turn and who you know will intercede with God on your behalf is a powerful source of hope, easing the discouragement that can so easily set in during times of stress.

Most long-term associate staff who are thriving in ministry report that they have one or more prayer partners who they share and pray with about their lives and ministries. In fact, more than 90 percent of all associates in our 2012 survey reported that having a prayer partner or partners enriches their ministries (up from 53 percent in 1997). These prayer partners can be members of the congregation, fellow associate staff members, peers in ministry in other congregations, or mentors in ministry. Different people bring different perspectives as we share with them and listen to them, but all can pray for us and our ministries. This is one of the most powerful sources of support we can receive from others. The associate staff members quoted below describe prayer partners who are a support in this way.

> I have five women who for the years I've been here have been my prime-time prayer support. I just went to them the other day and said, "I'm kind of dry." When I need a teacher, they pray. When I'm down, they pray. When I'm up, I share it with them. It's been a tremendous part of my ministry.
>
> —A CHILDREN'S PASTOR

> Having a personal prayer partner is important. I actually have two that are other gals, one my age and one much younger. Just to be absolutely transparent with them and then pray, cry with them, whatever. Confess or build them up, whichever is the need that week, but it means so much.
>
> —AN EDUCATIONAL MINISTRIES STAFF MEMBER

> I have prayer partners who are both females in ministry. Both of them have really been a support to me in ministry. Sometimes I need advice that's beyond my husband. My husband is so much my "choir" sometimes that he can't be objective. Sometimes I need to hear another point of view. And my prayer partners are very good. They're a very good balance, a good sounding board. Sometimes I tell them stuff I don't really want to tell my husband. And they know how to hold me up in prayer too.
>
> —A MINISTER OF CHRISTIAN EDUCATION

Support Group of Peers

Most thriving associate staff members have taken the initiative to participate in some form of peer support group. In general, these groups are made up of associate staff from churches in the community who have a similar focus of ministry (for example, children's ministry, youth ministry, music ministry, women's ministry). Group members gather regularly to share their lives and ministries and to offer support to each other. Some meet weekly or every two weeks; others get together monthly or every few months as their schedules allow.

However often they meet, the commitment is to support each other, not just to have some loosely organized community association or luncheon club.

Some groups function mainly as prayer support groups, as discussed above. Others serve as accountability groups, with members challenging each other to lives of integrity and faithful ministry. Such mutual discipleship requires a high level of trust and commitment. While members of such groups enjoy their open communication when they are together, they must be very cautious in sharing through various forms of social media, as confidences can be easily compromised in such environments. In spite of the potential risks of participating in such a group, the benefits for personal growth and enhanced ministry make it an attractive option for many.

The formation of intentional peer support groups is one of the most promising trends in associate staff ministry today. They have the potential of strengthening and encouraging thousands of associate staff members as they lead in their respective ministry areas. This ongoing support is critical for many if they are to ride the ups and downs of ministry. Many thriving associate staff members told how peer support groups affect their lives and ministries.

> In our area we started a little gathering of our children's ministries directors. . . . It's a group we can really talk with, talk to, we can share with. We feel it's confidential, it's to support one another. I think that group has been very good for me . . . when I thought I couldn't go on, just because they bring in a different perspective. They ask questions that help you to re-evaluate. It's been very good.
>
> —A CHILDREN'S PASTOR

> Having a support group of fellow DCEs is good, because in some ways it gets you out of your own denomination. You cross over. . . . Your thinking doesn't become just like in a box, like this is how we do it. There are other ways to do it. And it is nice to hear some refreshing ideas from other people and to know also that you could talk about some things that were kind of hard to go through without it really kind of getting to me.
>
> —AN EDUCATIONAL MINISTRIES STAFF MEMBER

When I was going through training through AME [African Methodist Episcopal] classes, it's a five-year program. We formed a coalition then, and we vowed that we would stick together regardless of what happened or where we went. When it came down to becoming elders, I believe there were six of us left. We're still very tight. We still call upon each other. There have been times, even personally, where we need someone to talk to, someone to cry with, someone to pray with. We all have problems, and we need someone to bounce it off of, and we've always been able to bounce it off with each other.

                                                    —AN ASSOCIATE PASTOR

Mentors as Models and Counselors

In research I conducted for my doctoral dissertation, early career clergy who were most satisfied in ministry enjoyed a relationship with a primary, older mentor along with a number of peer mentors. And we have found through our most recent survey that no matter how long veteran associate staff members have been in ministry, they continue to benefit from ongoing relationships with mentors (up from 51 percent in 1998 to 90 percent in 2012). In some cases, these primary mentors were instrumental in initially encouraging them to consider vocational ministry. Former pastors, children's or youth pastors, college or seminary professors—each can provide ongoing support and encouragement for the associate staff member in ministry. In other cases, mentors are peers with more experience serving in the same area of ministry who encouraged them after they got started. Some of these relationships began through participation in a local, regional, or national association for ministry professionals. Wherever they are found, the ongoing relationships with these mentors provide support through example, wise counsel, and words of encouragement. Many thriving associate staff members point to these mentors as one reason why they have made it so far in ministry.

I have monthly meetings with colleagues from other churches. A key issue is that while my supervising pastor may be very encouraging, he does not know much about my area of ministry. Having peers with whom I can interact and be mentored by is helpful.

—AN ASSOCIATE IN A LARGE CONGREGATION

I guess some of the guys that mentored me have been like a father to me—encouraging, comforting, urging me to live a life worthy. And I thought about some of the times I needed a shoulder to cry on and sometimes I needed encouragement and sometimes I needed a kick in the pants. And these guys always just seemed to have the wisdom to give me just what I needed at the moment. And they were very encouraging, or they would give a gentle nudge in the right direction. Encouragement from these guys, 'cause I knew they knew what they were talking about, it meant so much to me. They would see things in me that I didn't see in myself.

—A YOUTH PASTOR

The pastor and minister of music in the church where I felt my calling to the ministry have over the years been encouragers to me. It wasn't just when I made the decision, but for years afterwards [they] have kept in touch. They wanted to know how I was doing, just encouraging me along the way. When I had a need, I could call them. It has really meant a lot to me to have somebody who cared enough to see me start my ministry and encourage me to finish well.

—A MUSIC MINISTER

My college professor was key. She was the primary Christian education professor at this college that I attended, and she is now eighty-two years old. We still talk on the phone several times during the year. She is in Connecticut. But it was because she was real with me. It wasn't a classroom sterile setting. She had me in her home. It was the belief in me. I mean, I almost flunked teaching the Bible in her class because I was so quiet and shy, but she really believed in me. And now I teach college classes myself.

—A CHILDREN'S PASTOR

Extended Family as Support for Ministry

While immediate family relationships were the focus of chapter 4, some associate staff members find that the support of their extended family, especially their parents, is a blessing and helps them live out their ministry values and persevere during difficult times. In our 2012 study more than 90 percent of thriving associates reported extended family as a major source of encouragement. Maintaining healthy relationships with extended family increases the support to help us survive the hard times and find satisfaction as we serve. My wife and I have been enabled to minister to seminary alumni for the past twenty-one years due to extended family support through prayer, finances, and ongoing encouragement. Associate staff members who have this kind of support are blessed indeed. Two youth pastors told how their parents were an important support to them in ministry.

> For me it had to be my own parents. Fortunately, I was lucky enough to be born into a Christian family. But it wasn't just the churchgoing things. They were always very active and very God-fearing. I can't point to any one specific thing, but their support throughout the years, prayer support, and just their role model of ministering, serving, and caring.

> My parents still encourage me, and in times of discouragement they're on the phone and saying, "Hey, Mark, we know that God has called you into this, and we're praying for you." And they're a strong encouragement to me.

Considerations for Female Associate Staff

Women and men associate staff members have much in common, but they do have some different experiences in ministry. Because Kevin and I lack the experience of women associate staff, talking with women who have served in these roles for years and who are thriving in their ministries was a helpful learning experience for us. In addition to conducting focus groups with women associate staff (who made up almost 30 percent of the veteran survey respondents in the 1996–97 study), we enjoy the continued interaction with numerous female students and alumni who share with us their experiences in thriving as associates in various ministry settings. This is encouraging, since women have historically had a more difficult situation to deal with in vocational ministry. Women in associate staff positions have high-lighted a number of factors that make thriving in ministry more chal-lenging in some ways.

First, opportunities for women to serve on church staffs are often more restricted for both cultural and theological reasons. Some con-gregations or denominations limit women staff to certain ministry ar-eas, such as women's or children's ministry. Since many associate staff positions include a broader range of pastoral responsibilities, some churches prefer a man for these types of positions. This constraint can make locating an associate staff position more difficult for women than for men.

Second, even when women do find positions, they are often treated differently than male colleagues. Some congregations and de-nominations use the title *director* for female staff and *pastor* or *minister* for male staff members. Some also reserve ordination, or even li-censing, for men. This practice may reflect the more limited ministry responsibilities these women staff carry, with ordination and the title of pastor granted only to those who carry a broader pastoral role. It may also reflect a theological or cultural hesitancy to identify women officially as pastors. In other cases it may be the result of reserving ordination and the title *minister* or *pastor* for those who have earned a master of divinity degree; some women associate staff members do not have an MDiv. Whatever the reason, job titles are one way of conveying status in the Christian community, and ordination or li-censing can also provide some tax benefits that may not be available to many women staff.

Third, women occupy more of the part-time staff positions than men. For some women, serving part time can be a good way to stay involved vocationally in ministry while caring for the needs of their families. However, part-time positions have limited pay, and the work-hour demands frequently exceed the job description and pay received.

Fourth, more women than men in associate staff positions are sin-gle. While spouse and family support is beneficial in enabling associ-ate staff members to thrive in ministry, single associates lack that type of immediate, constant family support. In addition, single women may receive lower pay than their married male counterparts. With no spouse to bring in additional income, a woman may find it difficult to survive financially.

These and other unique challenges faced by female associates make it crucial for them to enjoy the blessings of supportive relationships within and outside the congregation, prayer partners, peer support groups, mentors, and extended family.

Taking Inventory: Questions for Reflection and Discussion

Every thriving associate staff member has his or her own unique mix of supportive relationships, and probably few would say that they have strong support in all six types of relationships. The issue is not the number of relationships or having some particular balance of the six types discussed above. Instead, it is about having access to high-quality supportive relationships that God can use to help sustain and encourage you in your ministry. You may have one or two such relationships, or many. The point is, we were not made to be alone, in either our ministry or our personal lives.

The following questions encourage you to look at the supportive relationships you already have and how you might draw encouragement from them. The questions also allow you to identify areas where supportive relationships could be developed, helping you move from surviving to thriving in ministry.

For Those in Preparation for Ministry or Newer Associate Staff Members

Friendships within the Congregation

1. To whom are you are being naturally drawn as you begin your ministry? Do you see potential for healthy relationships here? Any signs for caution?
2. What opportunities are there for you to observe potential friends in their native environment, outside the church ministry setting?
3. Are you allowing yourself to get to know people from across gender, generational, racial, or cultural boundaries?

Friendships outside the Congregation

1. What current friendships would be good for you to maintain as you prepare for and enter ministry? How can you ensure these relationships continue to grow?
2. What hobbies might you be able to enjoy with others outside your church? Are there organizations around that promote these activities?
3. Are there community groups (school, service organizations, civil government) where you can connect with potential friends who are not part of your congregation?

Prayer Partners

1. Whom do you know (or are you getting to know) that you could talk to about ministry or personal issues and who could pray with and for you?
2. Is there a classmate from your educational experience with whom you can continue a regular prayer and sharing relationship? How can you ensure it continues?

Support Group of Peers

1. Who are those current or former classmates that could serve as peers in your area of ministry? How could you connect and stay connected as your career or new ministry begins?
2. Is there a local, regional, or national professional organization for people in your type of associate staff ministry? If so, are you a member? If not, look over the types listed in appendix B. Could involvement in one of these kinds of organizations help you connect with others who share your motivation and concerns for ministry?
3. Have you investigated to see who in your community or region is involved in the same type of ministry as you? Might you provide leadership in forming such an alliance for mutual benefit?

Mentors

1. Who has been encouraging you as you begin to get involved in ministry? Are there pastoral staff, lay leaders, college or

seminary faculty who have been encouraging your growth and ministry involvement?

2. What areas of ministerial expertise are you most in need of? Who among your primary or peer mentors carries strengths in these areas? Would it be possible to renew or strengthen these contacts?

Extended Family

1. If you have parents or other extended family who encourage and support you in your ministry, have you thanked God and them for their support? Are you keeping them informed of your journey as you transition from your education or another ministry into the future?
2. If your extended family is not very supportive of your calling, what might you do to keep them informed while maintaining a positive relationship with them?

For Veteran Associate Staff Members

Friendships within the Congregation

1. What are your reflections concerning developing friendships in your congregation throughout the years? What have you learned through your experience?
2. Have you been able to develop meaningful friendships with people in your congregation? What helped that happen? What made it a challenge?
3. What are you doing to encourage congregational friends to maintain positive attitudes about the church and its leadership during times when you share with them some of your frustrations or discouragement?
4. How might you better integrate personal sharing, mutual encouragement, and prayer for one another as you work with lay leaders in your ministry area?

Friendships outside the Congregation

1. As you look back over your ministry years, how do you feel about the amount of time spent with people outside the congregation? What could you do to change that, if desired?

2. Have you enjoyed relationships that allow you a life outside your minister identity and responsibilities?
3. What community involvement have you found to be most rewarding and helpful in your experience? Is there need for a change in focus here?
4. How can you free up your schedule to allow for relationship building with those outside your ministry world? Is this even necessary, or do you feel good about your current experience?

Prayer Partners

1. As you think of those you share and pray with, are there ways you could be more disciplined and accountable with one another?
2. Are there other ways you can show support for your prayer partners (notes of encouragement, requests for updates, and so forth)?

Support Group of Peers

1. Have you enjoyed connecting with peers in your area about your work and issues you are facing? If this type of encouragement has not been a regular feature, what has hindered it? What steps could you take to make those connections now?
2. Are there areas in your life and ministry right now where you could use encouragement from a colleague to live out what you believe to be important and right?
3. What helpful peer relationships have you let slide over the years? How could you reconnect and rebuild that supportive network?

Mentors

1. What about people you have gotten to know through involvement in a ministerial or professional organization? Might it be beneficial to contact one or more of them to let them know how God has worked in and through your life, and invite them to respond?
2. Are there people who have mentored you in the past with whom you've lost touch? Consider getting in touch and telling them

about your life and ministry, thanking them for their investment in you. If you need their counsel and prayer, ask if they would be willing to encourage and assist you in these ways.

3. Are you serving as a primary or peer mentor for someone else? If not, can you think of some possible candidates?

Extended Family

1. If you have parents or other extended family who have continued to support you over the years, have you thanked them lately? How can you allow them to share in the joys and sorrows and to praise God with you?
2. Some of your family members might be more supportive if they knew more about your work. How might you inform and invite them to participate in your life's work (pray for specific items, share their wisdom with you regarding a certain issue, and so forth)?

Part 3

Thriving Professionally

Introduction

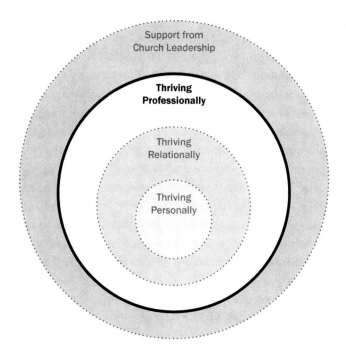

Thriving in ministry always involves an interaction between who we are (thriving personally), our relationships with others (thriving relationally), and how we respond to the ministry context we find ourselves in (thriving professionally). It is not just a matter of the particular challenges we face in our ministry setting but how we respond to those challenges, in both our attitudes and our actions, that makes a difference in our ability to thrive. Some ministry settings provide a more supportive environment in which to serve, others less so, but they can still be places of meaningful ministry. It is good for us to consider what contextual factors are most important for our ability to thrive in our work. In some cases we may be able to work within our setting to bring about the changes in our context that will help us thrive more. In other cases we may not be able to change them, but we can learn better ways to compensate for them and cope with the challenges we experience.

As Mick and I (Kevin) talked with veteran associate staff members, we heard them explain that at times their own attitudes and commitments helped them thrive in settings that were challenging. In chapter 7 we examine these commitments and attitudes, why they are important, and ways to cultivate them. We are not victims of our circumstances, but with God's grace we can rise to the challenge and keep a positive perspective on what we are facing. We can learn a lot from the thriving associate staff who shared with us.

Our ministry context, including work expectations and conditions, and church policies, can make it easier or harder to thrive. I served in three congregations in associate staff ministry, and in each one, some aspects made ministry there enjoyable and others made it frustrating. From the perspective of veteran associate staff members, what are the most important elements that help them thrive in their ministries? Chapter 8 identifies and discusses these elements, looking closely at why they have the impact they do and what can be done to change a situation if they are not present. We cannot change everything about our ministry setting, but we can develop at least a few aspects that will help us thrive as we serve.

Achieving a sense that we are thriving in our ministry does not guarantee we will feel that way forever. Sometimes we can go through a long season of thriving, only to find that something has changed and we no longer have that same feeling of well-being. In chapter 9 we ask, what can you do if you are not currently thriving? How can you determine what has brought about this change in your experience? Who might you turn to for help in sorting it out? What issues might you consider as you reflect on your experiences? Finally, if it seems that the situation cannot be changed, how can you determine whether you ought to consider a major change of ministry setting? This is not comfortable territory for any of us, so it is good to seek wisdom from veteran associate staff if you are wondering whether a move is needed or not.

Along with thriving personally and thriving relationally, thriving professionally is key to the overall experience of thriving in associate staff ministry. We trust that the practical wisdom shared in this section will be useful and encouraging as you serve where you are.

7

Attitudes and Commitments That Support Thriving

I have learned in whatever situation I am to be content. I know how to be brought low, and I know how to abound. In any and every circumstance, I have learned the secret of facing plenty and hunger, abundance and need. I can do all things through him who strengthens me.
—Philippians 4:11b–13

When I (Kevin) was a boy growing up, we lived in a farming area of upstate New York. Our ancient house, next door to a dairy farm, had a large, uneven lawn with lots of trees. When I reached the age of eleven, mowing the lawn became my responsibility. I hated it! The lawn just seemed to go on forever, and I swore most of it was uphill. We had a standard gas-engine push mower that I had to haul around, and I quickly tired of the novelty of it. I wanted to be out riding my bike and playing with friends or inside watching television.

Now, my father told me that the lawn could be mowed in about three hours, but I knew he had to be lying because it generally took me about six. Because he viewed this as one of my chores, and not an extra job, he offered me one dollar if I could get it all done in one day, but if it took me more than that I would receive nothing. I seldom collected that dollar in those early years. All the time I was mowing the lawn I kept longing to be somewhere else, doing something else. Almost any problem I ran into was enough to distract me from the task. Once I stopped, it was hard to get started again. If I ran out of gas, that was a good time for a break. If it sprinkled a little, I wouldn't mow anymore because the grass might clog up the mower. If a favorite TV program came on, I would be tempted to take a break to watch it. The more I fussed about the mowing, and the more I thought about how big and unending the job seemed, the slower I worked and the longer it took. I can remember once taking four days to complete the job, only to have to start all over again three days later.

Although I'm sure my father wondered at times if he had done the right thing in assigning this chore to me, the responsibility for mowing the lawn remained mine throughout my junior-high and high-school years. As the years went by, I found that when I had some activity coming up that I could do only if the mowing was done, I was motivated to work a little harder and faster. The faster I could get the job done, the less I dreaded it and the harder I worked. I began shaving the time it took to complete the job from six hours to five, and then to four, and finally to three. The job had not changed. It still involved the same large, uneven, hilly lawn and the same mower. What changed was my attitude, and that affected my ability to get the job done more quickly, which in turn affected my attitude toward the job. While I never looked forward to mowing the lawn, I no longer hated or dreaded it, and I found a measure of satisfaction in getting it done and doing it well.

My son, Nathan, attended a junior high school where the administration displayed a banner with a slogan for the students and faculty. The banner read, ATTITUDE IS EVERYTHING. While that slogan may be an overstatement, it trumpets an important truth. Our perspective on our circumstances, and the attitude we develop within them, is often much more important than the circumstances themselves. Some people, no matter how good their life or work circumstances, still find fault and complain. Others, no matter how bad their situations, remain thankful and hopeful. Our attitude affects our motivation, which in turn affects our energy level and ability to focus on the task and ignore distractions. A positive attitude enables us to persevere in the face of problems and find satisfaction in a task well done. A negative attitude can make even an easy task a draining chore. Our attitudes in turn affect the commitments we make, and sticking to our commitments help us weather some of the ups and downs of our changing attitudes. Both are important to help us work through issues on the job and continue to thrive in spite of our circumstances.

Interestingly enough, when long-term associate staff were asked what helped them thrive in their ministries, they did not just talk about work relationships, helpful practices, and job factors. They also spent a lot of time talking about their own attitudes and commitments and how these contributed to their ability to thrive amid the challenges of ministry.

Attitudes and Commitments for Thriving in Ministry

Thriving rather than merely surviving in associate staff ministries requires cultivating a number of attitudes and affirming and living out commitments. Long-term associate staff identified and described nine attitudes and commitments that help them thrive in ministry. As you read about them, consider the attitudes of your own heart and the nature and strength of your commitments in ministry. Ask yourself if you need to seek God's help in changing your attitudes and strengthening your commitments as you fulfill your ministry responsibilities.

Valuing Your Ministry Area

To stay with an area of ministry for many years and to find satisfaction in doing it, you need to feel that it is important. Nearly all the 2012 study participants report that their burden, passion, or vision for the ministry they are doing is a strong influence on their thriving in ministry over time. We all want to give ourselves to ministries that we see as significant, valuable to God and to God's people. We need to value our ministries enough to give them our best effort.

One long-term youth pastor described a change in his attitude that helped him move from simply *enjoying* what he did to *valuing* it.

> What kept me going in the early years was my love for kids and being able to do fun stuff. You know, being able to do a cool job. I would get up in the morning and say, "I like what I do. It's awesome, and I get paid for it." That's what it was like in the early years. Now, that stuff is still fun, but it's combined with seeing that these kids are lost souls. I knew they were before, but now as I mature I'm seeing the impact of my ministry. I see them as lost souls, and then I see the impact I'm having on the kids who come through the ministry now, and it's tremendous. That's what is giving me my second wind.

Also, the level of value our congregations attach to our areas of ministry can influence our attitudes as well. In a previous study in which I was involved about current and former associate staff members, one factor identified by many former staff members as contributing to their departure was the lack of support the church gave to their ministry area. They found this discouraging, making it hard to maintain their own motivation and energy for ministry. When you feel that you are in this kind of situation, it may still be possible to thrive, but having a supportive fellowship of people in your area of ministry is critical.

Contentment with Your Ministry Role

This attitude goes hand in hand with the first. It is hard to thrive in ministry if you find yourself wishing you were doing something else or serving somewhere else. It's hard to give yourself to your work if you find no real joy in doing it well. A spirit of contentment about being where you are, doing what you are doing is critical if you are going to find satisfaction in your ministry. While 84 percent of those in the 1998 study reported that this was influential in their thriving in ministry, this number has risen to 97 percent of the thriving associate staff in the 2012 study.

For many people, this point relates to their understanding of calling to ministry. If they are convinced of God's call to this kind of ministry, then it is easier to be committed to it and to find contentment in it over time. However, if their sense of calling is not clear, or if it is focused on some other type of ministry, then it is easy to view their current ministry involvement as a stepping-stone to the "real ministry." One long-term associate staff member described it this way:

> I think you have to see it not as a stepping-stone to a better career. I know a lot in our denomination for whom it's just like, "I'm going to be a youth pastor for *x* number of years and then I'm going to move on to the bigger things." But this is real ministry. I love my job. I'm a blessed man.

This spirit of contentment is especially important when serving in a less-visible ministry and being more of a support to the senior pastor. Being number two, three, or whatever on staff can test the humility level of some staff members. Maintaining the spirit of a servant and being content to serve others in the church and on staff through your ministry efforts can help you thrive in ministry over the years.

Even if your sense of calling in ministry is clear, your contentment can be undermined if you possess a spirit of pride or insecurity that leads you to seek greater recognition and praise from others. This kind of spirit can cause you to treat your ministry as a career with a ladder to climb to the top, instead of as a vocation that you fulfill where God places you. Little contentment awaits you if you treat it as a career, but much contentment is possible if you will relax and allow God to direct your ministry path. Eugene Peterson describes the dangers of viewing ministry as a career in *Under the Unpredictable Plant*.[1] These include such things as catering to a consumer church mentality, focusing on the size and prosperity of our congregations, a competitive spirit with other pastors, and pride. I had all my ministry practicum students read it when I taught that course, and we discussed the need for a vocational perspective on our ministries. I found it interesting that those students with the most years in ministry were the quickest to affirm the importance of this perspective. They knew the difference this point of view made in their own contentment in ministry.

A Spirit of Initiative

The vast majority of thriving associate staff members in our studies reported that they are self-starters in their work and do not need much supervision. Because of the nature of associate staff ministries, a lot of initiative rests with staff members in fulfilling their ministry obligations. To thrive in associate staff ministry, you need to combine a *spirit of cooperation*, so that you can work well as a member of the ministry team (this is discussed in chapter 5), and a *spirit of initiative*, so that you can give leadership in your own ministry area. This initiative shows up in five aspects of an associate staff member's work.

Managing yourself. As an associate staff member, you need to be a good self-manager. That is, you need to be able to discipline yourself to tackle the demands of the job without close oversight from your supervisor. Using your time and resources well, keeping track of details, and taking care of your own personal needs in the process allow you to function at your best. You cannot rely on someone else to do this for you; it is something each person must do on his or her own.

Developing a ministry philosophy. Take the initiative in developing a philosophy of ministry for your area. Your ministry philosophy guides and unifies your efforts, allowing you to concentrate on those things that are most productive for reaching your objectives. However, you need to fit your philosophy together with that of the whole church or you will find conflicts developing frequently. You need to learn about the ministry philosophy of the senior pastor, the church board, and the church as a whole so as to fit yours into the larger picture. This will allow you to support the ministry of the whole church through your own particular ministry area.

Equipping yourself for ministry. Take initiative also to equip yourself to fulfill your ministry responsibilities. Whatever level of education you have attained, your academic preparation did not address everything you will face in ministry. Much of what you need to know to minister effectively you will have to learn on the job. To thrive in ministry, recognize your strengths, weaknesses, and gaps in ministry preparation and find ways to equip yourself more fully. We'll discuss this subject in more detail later in this chapter.

Assessing ministry needs and effectiveness. Initiative is needed in assessing ministry needs and evaluating current ministry strategy effectiveness. These responsibilities rest with you if you have taken on leadership responsibilities as an associate staff member. You may want to make this assessment cooperatively with other staff members, but it needs to be done if you are going to give leadership in your ministry area.

Initiating change. In light of the ministry needs identified, you need to be able to initiate change in your ministry area. Thriving in ministry is partly a by-product of seeing ministry successes and finding satisfaction in them. In taking initiative to achieve greater effectiveness in your ministry area, your satisfaction will increase as you see what God does through your efforts and the efforts of those with whom you work.

Patience and Perseverance

Associate staff ministries, whatever the area of responsibility, are seldom smooth sailing for long. Sometimes perseverance and patience are needed to overcome challenges or problems. As a ministry leader, you may see the need for change before others do, and you may become impatient waiting for others to recognize and respond to the needs you see. Having patience and being able to persevere in the face of obstacles and disappointment are critical for longevity in ministry, leading to the satisfaction that longevity can bring. Nearly all the participants in our studies identified this as an important personal characteristic for thriving. One associate staff member described her experience this way:

> I have always had that personality that you start something and you finish it. Even when there are tough times, you just stick it through. You persevere. It's not going to be easier anywhere else, and you need to work this out. I've made a commitment to this place, and I'm going to do everything I can and make it work until I've exhausted everything.

Patience and perseverance are especially important as we face conflicts with others with whom we work, whether supervisors, fellow associate staff, or lay leaders in our ministry area. Unresolved conflict is one major contributor to associate staff members' leaving their positions. Staff members who are patient, who persevere through the unpleasantness of conflict with their supervisors or others, and who find a way to resolve it are then freed to focus their efforts again on the ministry they enjoy. While this book is not an attempt to address conflict resolution in any exhaustive way, a couple of foundational tips can, I believe, make it easier for you to persevere and find a way through the conflict.

Adopt a spirit of humility that is not defensive but open to criticism and willing to listen and to receive correction. Even if you are convinced that the person you disagree with is wrong, that does not make you right! And, even if you are right, that does not mean you are presenting your ideas in a way to win a hearing. If you come across as arrogant, prideful, or unwilling to listen to others' ideas, you may shut down effective dialog and collaboration.

Maintain respect for those you are in conflict with, loving them and committing yourself to working together as a team. Christ prayed for our unity and love for each other (John 14, 17). Paul reminds us of the unity we have in the Spirit and encourages us to live it out (1 Cor. 12, Phil. 2, Eph. 4).

As difficult as ministry can be, these two things need to characterize our attitudes and commitments as we patiently work through conflict and strive for unity in ministry together.

Valuing Longevity in Ministry

A commitment on the part of associate staff to long-term ministry in their present setting reinforces stability and contentment and helps the staff member deal with frustrations, challenges, and tempting job offers. This commitment is not a stubborn refusal to consider new ministry opportunities God may guide you to but a commitment to serve where you are until God makes clear that a change is needed. Fully 98 percent of participants in the 2012 study identified this as highly influential in their ability to thrive in ministry.

This commitment overlaps to some degree the development of patience and perseverance, but it is more than an attitude or personality characteristic. It is a decision to stay put that can encourage you to grow and mature in your ministry setting and begin to see the fruit that longevity can bring. So much of the spiritual fruit of our ministries is slow growing and requires time before we can see what lasts and what does not. When we make frequent moves, we do not see the long-term impact of our ministry, and we miss out on some deep joys that await us. One youth pastor recalled that when he came to his present congregation, he made a commitment to stay at least until the seventh graders had graduated from high school. He wanted to see their growth and knew that wouldn't be possible if he left after a couple of years. Others say their greatest joys in ministry come from seeing people mature in their own ministries and seeing kids grow up into adults who love God and serve others.

A commitment to longevity in ministry makes you think twice before giving up on a frustrating situation. We all feel like quitting at times, and a strong commitment to longevity helps us work through the conflicts or frustrations we face. There may come a time when a change is best, but a bias toward longevity can help us discern when this is truly the case and not just a temptation to move to a higher paying or more prestigious position. The opportunity for more pay and greater recognition for our work are not bad things in themselves, but these factors can make it more challenging to discern when God wants us to stay where we are and when it is appropriate to move on.

Desire for Continued Growing and Learning

To thrive in ministry requires the willingness and ability to grow, learn, and change to be better equipped for our ministry demands, especially when they are changing over time. For example, the youth pastor who starts working with a group of twenty kids and finds the group growing to fifty needs to learn how to develop, supervise, and support lay leaders to meet the demands of an expanding ministry. Or again, the music minister who begins working with the adult choir and finds a number of members interested in forming a small group within the choir for spiritual growth and encouragement may need to learn more about giving leadership to that kind of ministry.

Ministry opportunities and demands will change, and you need to commit yourself to keeping pace with the changing needs around you. Over and over again, long-term associate staff members who are thriving in their ministries point to the importance of continuing education and professional enrichment. More than 95 percent of the thriving staff members in these studies identified professional growth as very important to their ability to thrive in ministry. One minister of music had this to say:

> I've noticed something that has caused other ministers of mu-
> sic to fall by the wayside: It's not being open to change and
> growing on a constant basis. That's one of the reasons why I
> attend MusiCalifornia every year. I don't miss it unless I have
> to. And it's a constant growing experience, constantly chang-
> ing, new techniques, or methods. If you're not willing to do it,
> then the ministry leaves you behind.

There are a variety of ways to keep growing and learning in ministry. Over half of those who participated in this study belong to a professional association and attend regular conferences or other meetings where they learn from others, develop networks together, and receive encouragement in their ministry. Others read relevant ministry journals and books, looking for new ideas that might be beneficial in their ministry setting. Still others attend seminars, workshops, or courses at seminaries or universities that address issues they face in their work. Whatever the venue, the commitment to keep learning, growing, and remaining open to change is important for ministry effectiveness and satisfaction over time.

Valuing People over Programs

Again and again, thriving associate staff members described the need to stay focused on the people served, not on the programs or activities they organize and run. This is an almost universal perspective and one that helps associate staff thrive even when programmatic problems arise. While a smoothly running program can provide some limited measure of satisfaction, it is nothing compared to the power of seeing God work in people's lives. Associate staff who put too much focus on the programmatic demands of their ministries can miss out on one of the deepest sources of satisfaction available to them. One youth pastor explained it this way:

> I've seen a lot of youth pastors through the years, and one of the things that keeps me going is that long-term vision that goes beyond the numbers, that you're here to change lives. And that takes time. I think most of us have been there, we can get a hundred kids there next week if we want to. But I've seen too many of my friends or people that I've known get into youth ministry, and they burn out because it is a numbers game for them. The ones that I know that have lasted and have made a difference over the years have been the ones with that vision that we're going to change lives, not just get numbers.

Again, this focus relates to your understanding of your calling from God. Our calling is not to run programs but, through the various programs and relationships we oversee, to encourage people to come to faith in Jesus Christ and to become more Christlike. When we lose sight of the end, the satisfaction we gain from the means is not enough to enable us to thrive in ministry. The problem is that amid the daily demands of overseeing ministry programs, it is easy to fall into a program-focused mind-set. It takes discipline, commitment, and frequent reminders to keep our focus on the people we serve.

Investing in Others

In our 2012 study, 95 percent of the associate staff reported that mentoring others in ministry contributed to their own ability to thrive. In addition, more than 70 percent reported volunteering for ministry outside their local church, helping with community, professional, or denominational ministry efforts. These types of outside involvement contributed to their overall satisfaction. Thriving in ministry is the result not just of doing your own immediate job well but also of allowing God to stretch you and teach you as you invest in others and find opportunities to serve beyond your congregation.

The commitment to invest in others may be especially relevant for associate staff who have been in ministry for several years. Once we have developed some measure of effectiveness in an area of ministry we value, we can shift our focus to supporting others who are investing themselves in the same ministry area. For example, an experienced minister of music may look for ways to encourage and support newer ministers of music as they get started in ministry. A children's pastor described providing internship opportunities for students:

> I appreciate the belief in internship within our church, and I have the privilege of interning young men and women and really supporting them. We say the children are the future, but some of us are getting older in life, and we can't wait for the children to grow up. We need to be producing the next generation of young adults that will have the same passion for ministry with children that we have.

Another associate pastor told how she was affected by a denominational school's approaching her congregation to help equip students for ministry:

> I know that as I'm beginning to mentor, as I see and meet with a lot of young ministers, I pick up on their energy, and I help them avoid a lot of those pitfalls that I fell into. I think this also helps me stay on the cutting edge of what's happening.

Being involved in ministry opportunities outside your own congregation can be an energizing experience. It can enable you to rub
shoulders with others with similar commitments and passions, to encounter and share your faith with those who are unchurched in your
community, to contribute to the ministries of other churches, and to
live out your ministry priorities in a larger setting. All these can stimulate you to reassess your ministry efforts, your calling from God, and
the positive aspects of your own congregational setting.

Supporting Your Supervisor

Making a commitment to support your supervisor and his or her
ministry success, consistently communicating this to the supervisor,
and daily living it out serve to build trust and mutual commitment
between associate staff and supervisor. This bond strengthens your
ability to work well together, making your joint ministry experience
more rewarding and satisfying. This supports thriving in ministry for
both supervisor and associate staff. Fully 97 percent of the thriving
associate staff in our 2012 study say this is an important commitment
for them and that it has a moderate influence on their ability to thrive
in their ministry.

We described in chapter 5 supervisors' need for loyalty from their
associate staffs. Your loyalty and commitment go hand in hand. For
some people, loyalty means standing by one's supervisor when he is
criticized and not contradicting his decisions in public settings. Commitment may cover some of the same behaviors, but it includes a
positive, active role of supporting and helping your supervisor for
his maximum effectiveness in ministry. It also means caring for your
supervisor as a person, praying for him and doing what you can to
encourage him in ministry. This kind of commitment helps build a
spirit of partnership and increases the satisfaction you can find in ministering together.

Taking Inventory: Questions for Reflection and Discussion

Together, these nine attitudes and commitments provide a strong base
for encouraging longevity, satisfaction, and well-being in ministry.
They can help create the context for thriving in ministry. Here are

some questions you may want to reflect on or discuss with others to help you evaluate your situation. They may also trigger other questions that would be helpful to consider. While most of these questions are written with the experienced associate staff member in mind, they also can be profitable for the new or "wannabe" associate staff member to reflect on as preparation for handling the stresses of ministry leadership.

1. If you could put your time and efforts into any ministry, what would you do? How does it compare with the ministry responsibilities you carry now or are considering taking on? If there is a significant difference between what you would like to do and what you are now doing, why is that? If you are considering a position, how much of what you want to do needs to be in the job mix for you to find that ministry role satisfying? What do you think God would have you do in the near future?

2. Probably all associate staff members have considered quitting their staff positions and going off to do something else. When do these kinds of thoughts tend to cross your mind? If you have seriously thought of doing something else, what is it? Why have you not gone in that direction? Again, what do you think God would have you do in the near future?

3. What contributes to or undermines your ability to find contentment in life in general and in your ministry specifically? What help do you need in dealing with things that make it hard to be content? To whom could you turn for help, either now or in the future, if this becomes an issue for you?

4. Do you find it easy to take initiative in ministry, or do you prefer to have more direction from your ministry supervisor? Do you sense a discrepancy between the level of initiative that you prefer to take and the level that is acceptable to others in your ministry setting? What changes would you have to make to resolve this tension? If you are a candidate for a position, how might you explore this with your potential supervisor?

5. Have you found yourself frequently impatient or frustrated over problems in your ministry area in your present role? How do you deal with these feelings? In the past, have you persevered through a ministry difficulty and seen God work it out?

What have you learned from that experience? What might you do to grow in patience as you face ministry challenges now or in the future? To whom might you turn for help with this issue?

6. When you have found yourself in conflict with a ministry supervisor or someone else in your ministry area in the past, what problems have you encountered in trying to resolve it? As you examine your own reactions to conflict, what attitudes and actions have helped you work through the conflict, and which ones have made that harder to do? What help do you need in handling conflicts better? What can you do to get that help?

7. What are you now doing to keep learning and growing in ministry? What resources are you aware of that you have not yet investigated and tried? Where would you like to start, and what encouragement or accountability do you need to see this plan through? How can you ensure this does not get crowded out of a busy ministry schedule?

8. How easy has it been for you to lose focus on the people you minister to and to focus on the program aspect of your work? If this has been or is a problem for you, what can you do to remind yourself of the purposes you strive to accomplish and the importance of the people you serve?

9. If your ministry is going fairly well and you think you have some time and energy you can invest in other ways, have you found any opportunities in your community, denomination, or profession to make a contribution? What opportunities can you explore? Is there an individual you might be a support to and possibly mentor as he or she begins in ministry?

10. What is your feeling about committing to serve in your present setting for a long time? What problems or benefits do you see? What indications do you have from God about your future ministry? What would it take for you to seriously consider leaving your current staff position? What would it take to keep you where you are?

11. In what ways are you communicating your commitment and support to your ministry supervisor? Is there anything that makes such communication difficult? If so, is this barrier serious enough to cause you to question whether you should

continue in this staff position? Is there someone with whom you should discuss this difficulty, seeking wise counsel on how to proceed? If you have done anything to cause your supervisor to question your support, what steps do you think you need to take to improve the situation?

8

Ministry Settings That Support Thriving

Let the elders who rule well be considered worthy of double honor,
especially those who labor in preaching and teaching. For the Scripture
says, "You shall not muzzle an ox when it treads out the grain," and,
"The laborer deserves his wages."

—1 TIMOTHY 5:17–18

So if there is any encouragement in Christ, any comfort from love, any
participation in the Spirit, any affection and sympathy, complete my
joy by being of the same mind, having the same love, being in full ac-
cord and of one mind.

—PHILIPPIANS 2:1–2

One simple answer to the question of how to thrive in associate staff ministry is, find a great church setting to serve in. We're all tempted to think that our ministry frustrations and problems would disappear if only we could find the right congregation. However, there *is* no perfect congregational setting. Each has its unique mixture of challenges and blessings. Even if a perfect setting existed, that would not necessarily ensure that we would thrive in ministry there. We each have our unique gifts, personalities, limitations, and needs. Each of us has areas in which God wants us to grow. Some of that growth will come through challenges and difficult situations, not from having an easy ministry.

I (Kevin) served in three different church contexts as an associate staff member. Each of them had elements that helped support me in my ministry and encouraged me in the midst of ministry challenges. Even though this was true, and I am grateful for that support, one congregation was such a challenging ministry context that over time I experienced deep discouragement and questioned my call to ministry. I found another to be challenging in different ways, but aspects of the ministry there energized me and helped me experience a stronger sense of contribution in my service, helping me to thrive in spite of the challenges. My third ministry setting was a great place to thrive in ministry. The ministry challenges were no less, but the support system and climate that God used to encourage and sustain me was stronger, helping me thrive in the midst of the challenges. All these settings had their challenges, but my ability to thrive improved in some settings more so than in others.

Now, I don't believe that we should seek problem-free congregation. It seems to me that God calls us, imperfect servant leaders, to serve an imperfect church, helping it and us grow toward maturity in Christ. But as we serve, the church is called to join us and support and honor us in our ministry (1 Tim. 5:17, 18). Each setting has aspects that encourage us in ministry, making it easier to thrive, and situations that are stressful or discouraging, making thriving more difficult. Whether or not your congregation has all the features you would like to make your ministry easy and enjoyable, I do believe that it is possible for you to take the initiative and make some adjustments that will help you move toward thriving.

While the previous chapter addressed the attitudes and commitments that associate staff members need to foster if they are to thrive, it seems evident that some ministry settings are more difficult than others. When long-term associate staff members reflected on the effect of their church environments, twelve aspects stood out as making a difference. These are discussed below under three major categories: characteristics of the congregation you serve in, characteristics of the staff position itself, and qualities of support from the church. Then we will examine the characteristics you may want to look for when you are a candidate for a church staff position and what steps you can take to improve the ministry setting in which you now serve.

Characteristics of the Church

Long-term associate staff described common characteristics of the churches where they thrived in ministry. These staff members' circumstances differed, and not every associate staff member felt that his or her church had to have all these characteristics for them to flourish, but the general picture holds. What we heard from those in our studies was that a healthy and growing congregation that supports your ministry area and accepts new ideas and ministry approaches and whose lay leaders are committed and dependable is a great place to thrive in ministry.

A Healthy and Growing Congregation

At a foundational level, when a church is functioning in a healthy way, ministry of any kind is less stressful and difficult for those in leadership, including associate staff members. Comparing survey responses from 1998 to 2012, the importance of this characteristic stayed high, but the percent of thriving associate staff who identified it as influential rose from 88 to 97 percent. Clearly, thriving in ministry is easier in a healthy ministry context. This is not to suggest that associates should avoid serving congregations that have problems or look for a new position if difficulties arise. Instead, helping their church become healthy should be a goal to strive for. Everyone in the church will reap the benefits in their ministries when the church is healthy.

A healthy congregation is characterized by a sense of unity in Christ (John 17:20–21); an evident love for God and for others, especially for fellow disciples of Jesus Christ (John 13:34–35; Luke 10:25–28); and the opportunity for all to exercise their gifts in ministry, building up the body of Christ (Eph. 4:11–16). A healthy church is characterized by unity in ministry vision and by church members who use their gifts to strengthen the body in its pursuit of that vision. It is also marked by patience, love, and forgiveness when disagreements or offenses between members arise. Political maneuvering is discouraged, and people are able to work through hurts and disagreements without bitterness gaining a foothold. While no congregation may fully and consistently exhibit these qualities, if these are valued by church leaders and present to some degree, the congregation has the opportunity to grow toward greater health. This health in turn makes all ministries and leadership duties easier. Time and energy are not spent on damage control but used to extend the church's outreach and ministries.

Support for Your Ministry Area

When a congregation values and supports a staff member's area of ministry, the staff member is likely to feel that what he or she is doing is significant. We all want to give our time and effort to tasks of importance. Nearly all the 2012 survey respondents who were thriving in their ministries reported that this was one of the stronger factors that made thriving possible. While our basic understanding of the importance of our ministries comes from God, the support of others in the church gives an added boost that can help us persevere in the face of difficulties and calm the nagging doubts that maybe we should be doing something else more important. When verbalized support becomes practical action, it can provide us with the resources needed for successful ministry. Support for a ministry area can be shown in a number of ways. One is the encouragement and prayer support of lay leaders. One music minister explained:

> Having a board that believes in you is extremely helpful—instead of just accounting to them, having them support you. When you're called to a board meeting, when normally you're not there, usually you panic. But then you find out they just want to know about your ministry that night and pray for you. It's so affirming.

Support can be communicated also through budget allocations for planned activities, opportunities for staff to discuss ministry issues with church leaders, and occasions for staff to communicate with the congregation about their ministry areas. One youth pastor described the support he experienced at his church.

> Another thing that has been very, very important to me is being in a church that's supportive of youth ministry, not just in theory, but very much so in practice. They let the youth pastor be a part of the elder board, recognized as a vital person. I've been involved in churches that allow the youth pastor to have pulpit time to be able to share the vision of youth ministry and then financially backing up the programs and the kind of weird ventures that we want to participate in with our kids. That's been really helpful. . . . Talking to a lot of people who are close to burnout or whatever, I keep hearing from them over and over that "I just don't feel like the church has really supported the youth ministry here." I've been fortunate to be on the opposite side of that.

Knowing that the congregation believes in and supports the ministry into which you are pouring your energy is a boost when the going gets rough and discouragement nags at you. Sometimes the support is there but we're not aware of it. It may take initiative on your part to communicate with others about your ministry—pastoral staff, board members, and lay leaders—so that their support for it can grow and become more evident to you.

Openness to New Ideas and Approaches

Thriving associate staff members report that their churches allow them to exercise leadership and creativity in their ministry areas. Of those who participated in our 2012 study, 96 percent identified this as having influence on their ability to thrive in ministry. Most associates want to be able to evaluate the ministries they are responsible for and lead in making them more effective. They want to be ministry leaders, not just program maintainers. A congregation that is open to ministry assessment and new ideas offers a supportive environment for the creative associate staff member to take risks and try out new ministry approaches without fearing that failure will result in rebuke or diminished congregational support. This freedom may come more easily once the congregation and lay leadership observe the associate's commitment and faithful ministry over time. Others may be ready for new ideas right away, because they see that what they have been doing is not effective. What matters is that there is an openness to consider new approaches to ministry as we assess our current efforts. One children's pastor described his church's openness:

> The church is a healthy church, and it's a growing church, and so it's a very enjoyable environment to work in. They are willing to try new things. But if you try something and you fail, that's OK. We pull up our socks and move on, and try something else the next time. So it's very innovative. I think of all of us on staff as entrepreneurs in our areas.

Committed and Dependable Lay Leaders

One great encouragement to associate staff members is lay leaders who demonstrate commitment to their own ministry responsibilities.

These people become partners, working together to strengthen the congregation's ministries. Nearly all those we heard from who are thriving in ministry identified this as an important factor for them. Committed lay leaders strengthen the commitment of church staff. When lay leaders are faithful and dependable in their ministries, they make the work of associate staff members easier. This commitment by congregational members reduces the stress that comes with vocational ministry.

One of our interviewees shared how important this was for him. In Brian's ten years on church staffs, he has deeply appreciated the lay leaders with whom he has worked closely. Many of them have been faithful, going the extra mile to see that needs are met, and dependable in attending meetings when there were ministry issues to resolve. Their commitment in the face of competing life demands has inspired him in his ministry. They have been a source of joy, helping Brian persevere when things were not going smoothly. The few times when some lay leaders proved undependable were extremely frustrating and discouraging. He was fortunate that those occasions were infrequent.

Characteristics of the Staff Position

The associate staff members we surveyed and interviewed identified three aspects of their positions as helping them thrive. We find it interesting that two have more to do with involvement beyond one's initial ministry responsibilities than with the demands of the job itself. The other has to do with the ability to focus your efforts on the ministry area you are most passionate about. The ability to thrive in ministry is enhanced by opportunities to fine-tune the job description over time and to give input into the broader scope of the church's ministries.

A Dynamic, Changing Position Description

As associate staff members serve in their positions for many years, they value opportunities to grow and take on new responsibilities. Ninety-two percent of our 2012 study participants identified this as a factor that contributed to their thriving in ministry over the years.

One director of Christian education said new challenges have served as a catalyst for growth in his life and ministry: "Challenges? Sometimes we look at them as added responsibility to an already crowded job, but the challenge—you do thrive because you have to rise to the occasion, and you can grow again professionally and personally."

Many associate staff appreciate the variety of tasks and challenges. Over time, as new challenges come, God draws out new gifts for ministry. It is not unusual for staff members to discover that they are good at and enjoy assignments that they had not considered when they first entered vocational ministry. This kind of growth on the job increases the ways that a staff member can serve the church. When congregations provide for times of evaluation and ministry needs assessment that can lead to adjustments in staff job descriptions, they encourage staff to blossom in ministry and find satisfaction in how God is directing and growing their gifts and abilities.

Opportunity for Input into the Church's Broader Ministry

When an associate staff member invests time and energy in ministry in a congregation, he or she naturally develops concern for the church and its broader ministries. In addition, the longer an associate staff member serves a church, the more opportunities he or she has to gain insight into the church, the community, and the ministry opportunities and obstacles. As this concern and insight grow, staff members need an opportunity to share what they are seeing and learning, a chance to help make a positive difference. Thriving associate staff members reported that they had opportunities in their staff positions to give input to ministry decisions outside their specific ministry responsibilities. This expression of confidence in their leadership contributed to their thriving in their ministries.

Opportunities for input come in a variety of ways. Some associate staff members are able to attend church administrative board meetings and discuss ministry issues there. Others do not attend this type of board meeting but discuss broad ministry issues at staff meetings with the senior pastor. Whatever the setting, the chance to help the congregation beyond one's specific job focus is a rewarding experience that raises the motivation and commitment to minister faithfully.

Opportunity to Focus on a Ministry Area of Passion

At the same time that associate staff value the opportunity to give input into the broader ministry of the church as part of the leadership team, and their positions may require them to oversee more than one ministry area in the congregation, most value being able to focus the bulk of their efforts in the ministry areas they care most deeply about. In our most recent survey, 87 percent of our thriving respondents said this contributed to their ability to thrive in ministry, though it was not as strong a factor as some others we have already discussed.

I know that in my own ministry experience, my sense of calling to lead the educational ministries of the church was so strong that I resisted attempts to broaden my ministry responsibilities to address other important ministry areas. Eventually, this led me to conclude that if the congregation really needed someone who could address the broader ministry needs and could not add another staff member to do this, then I should look for a new church to serve in the areas for which I was called, gifted, and trained. I knew that the church leadership saw broader responsibilities needing to be addressed that would not fit me well, lowering my effectiveness in ministry and draining me in the process. It was not a case of selfishly refusing to adapt but recognizing my calling and gifting. It would not have been good in the long run for either the church or myself, and I had to move on to allow the church to have the staff they needed. In this case, the church leadership and I chose to prayerfully investigate other options, and three days after I left to begin ministry in another congregation, their new associate pastor arrived. God provided for us both, helping me grow in my confidence of God's calling and provision.

Support from the Church

Chapters 5 and 6 in this book explore more fully the ways in which supportive relationships with pastoral and lay leaders help associate staff members persevere and thrive in ministry. A supportive congregational environment makes a big difference for staff. Communication with a supportive church board, adequate pay and benefits to provide for one's family, opportunities for continuing education, flexibility in the work schedule to address family needs, and positive feedback from members all enhance the ministry experience of associate staff members.

Communication with a Supportive Church Board

Although not all associate staff members attend meetings of their congregation's governing board, opportunities to meet with board members and to receive their encouragement and support can make a difference in a staff member's ability to thrive in ministry. Roughly three-fourths of the thriving associate staff in our 1998 study and over half of those in the 2012 study do attend administrative board meetings. This provides them the opportunity to share what is happening in their areas of ministry as well as to hear about the initiatives, needs, and issues the board is dealing with that may have an impact on their ministries. It also allows them the opportunity both to be encouraged by and to offer support to the board in its work. For associate staff members who do not attend such board meetings, finding other ways to communicate with the board is important. One youth pastor described how his senior pastor helps him.

> I think a good relationship with your board is important. It always makes me feel so good when the pastor comes out of the board meeting and says, "You need to know that the board said this," or "They agreed to pay for this," or something like that, because they felt what I was doing was worthwhile. It was valuable. That has really helped me.

Other churches establish a system whereby board members are matched up with associate staff members to learn more about them, the ministries they oversee, and what they need to carry out their ministries well. This kind of connection to the board is invaluable to many. One director of Christian education described his church's approach:

> We had a setup where they assigned elders to each pastoral staff member for a year or so. Not [to] supervise you, but as a friend, somebody that worked with you. And that was really supportive. I think I had an elementary principal one year,

and then another time a vice principal of a high school. Boy, those guys understood administration and education. We really clicked. We met every week for talk and prayer. Those were some significant years when I had the right kind of elder working with me.

An associate pastor explained how this linkage worked in his congregation and how it benefited him in practical ways.

> Within the structure of our elders' board, they have set up a liaison with each of the staff people. I've been very blessed to have very wonderful, caring liaisons. They meet with me once a month, and they open the door for me to express whatever it is that I'm dealing with—the good, the bad, the ugly. They support me, and if need be, . . . take it as an issue to the elders' board if it needs some action that requires their endorsement. They have addressed salary, benefit packages—you know, different things like that. I mean they will deal with those issues that can't seem to be brought up elsewhere.

However it is carried out, the opportunity to share with the board about one's ministry area and to receive encouragement and affirmation in return is a positive motivator for perseverance and faithfulness in ministry.

Adequate Pay and Benefits to Provide for Family

It is pretty safe to say that people who pursue associate staff ministry do not do so to accumulate wealth. There are far too many other vocations to choose from that pay much better. But while money is not a major motivator for associate staff members, it can affect their long-term contentment and stress level, even causing some to reluctantly seek other means of employment. One primary concern of church staff members is the ability to provide for the physical needs of themselves and their families (if married). Ninety percent of our study participants, both in 1998 and in 2012, identified this as a factor that helped them thrive over time in ministry.

Because the cost of living varies across North America, the family needs of associate staff members vary. In addition, the benefits packages that congregations provide differ so much that it is impossible to identify what level of salary would be adequate for associate staff in different contexts. One helpful rule of thumb is to look at the compensation of schoolteachers in your community with comparable education and experience. Your church may not be able to match that scale exactly, but if it can come close, you may find that with other benefits available (such as favorable tax status for housing expenses for licensed or ordained ministers) you are able to provide adequately for your family. Don't forget to consider the benefits package that the congregation is able to provide. Health and life insurance, ministry expense reimbursement, and retirement program contributions are other ways that a church can meet the needs of its staff members, helping them feel valued and supported.

Opportunities for Continuing Education

Overwhelmingly, thriving associate staff members report that part of what helps them thrive in ministry is the growth that takes place through their participation in continuing-education activities. Eighty-four percent of associate staff in our 1998 and 2012 studies identified this as influential in their thriving in ministry. These study participants report a wide range of activities that help them continue to learn and grow. For some it is as simple as having a friend or a small group of peers who read the same ministry-oriented book and discuss it together. Others find participation in professional association conferences and workshops beneficial. The benefits of attending these kinds of events can be both professional and personal. One music minister described her congregation's support for continuing education: "The first thing that comes to mind that my church does that helps me is their encouragement for personal growth. We're encouraged to go to conferences and workshops, schools, and stuff like that so we can grow in both professional and personal ways."

Still others have the opportunity to enroll in formal course work toward the completion of a higher-education degree that benefits their ministry practice. One children's pastor wrote about her decision to return to school for a master's degree in Christian education and the flexibility in schedule that her church allowed to make it possible: "Just the freedom to be able to get additional education while I could still work full time has been beneficial. I don't have to cut back hourly, but I can stay and work full time, and work on my master's program."

You may not have the opportunity to pursue a degree, but having support and encouragement to find ways to grow will help stretch and challenge you. It will help you avoid falling into a ministry-maintenance rut, giving you new perspectives, ideas, and models for ministry. If the money is available, attending courses or national professional conferences can be very encouraging and beneficial. If the money is not available for these kinds of events, then having time to meet with other ministry leaders in your area to discuss journal articles or books you have read and common ministry issues can be a stimulus to your ongoing development and growth.

Women Associate Staff and Continuing-Education Opportunities

Over 90 percent of both male and female thriving associate staff members attend professional conferences, conventions, or other educational events for continuing education and for networking with others in their area of ministry. Though both men and women reported that such events are a very influential factor in their ability to thrive in ministry over the years, women staff members rated these experiences as more influential than did the men. This rating may be due in part to differences in educational opportunities for some men and women associate staff members. Continuing-education events may help some women address ministry issues that they have not previously had the chance to study. It may also reflect the value of these settings for women as a place to make contact with other women in ministry and to develop supportive networks that extend beyond the educational event. Whatever the reasons, the experience of women associates is that these kinds of continuing-education events are a source of help in their ministries, improving their ability to thrive. It may be helpful for you to look actively for continuing-education events in your ministry area and to submit a request to your supervisor and church board for the time and financial support to attend. Try to make this a regular part of your ministry schedule, and use these events not only to gain knowledge and skills for ministry but also to connect with others in ministry and to strengthen your network of supportive relationships.

Flexible Work Schedule to Address Family Needs

There are few real perks to vocational ministry, but one of those that is deeply appreciated by associate staff members is the freedom to make adjustments in their work schedule to meet family needs, both their immediate family and their extended family. While some people might expect this to be an issue only for working mothers, both men and women associate staff members value this flexibility, especially in light of the evening demands that ministry responsibilities require. Fully 98 percent of our study participants in 2012 identified this as contributing to their ability to thrive in ministry. One minister of music described how such flexibility helped him and his family.

> We're going on a staff retreat next week, so I needed to move all my meetings to the same week, rather than spread them out. I had a Monday night meeting, a Tuesday night meeting, and a Wednesday night rehearsal, and I had a Sunday night Bible study. By Thursday morning, my three boys were in chaos. My wife was stressed, so I didn't go to work yesterday morning. I stayed home and cleaned the house, did the dishes, that sort of stuff.

Flexibility in schedule can also be seen as a sign of trust, a vote of confidence in the dependability of the associate staff member to do his or her work well. As with other signs of trust, this privilege may need to be earned over time as dependability and good judgment are demonstrated. A youth pastor shared what this trust meant to him and his family.

> I like the flexibility of the schedule. I'm respected as an expert in my area, and I don't have somebody bird-dogging me. We have set hours, but if I need to run off and do something, it's OK. My wife is in school right now and we have a little one. There are times when I have had to run home early, or pick my wife up, or even get somebody from the bus station. Nobody hassles me. They just realize that I'm competent and I'm not missing anything.

Women Associate Staff and the Flexible Work Schedule

In our surveys, while both men and women rated having a flexible work schedule as beneficial to their thriving in ministry, women rated it higher than did the men. Among the realities facing many women in associate staff ministry are the competing demands of caring for family and fulfilling ministry obligations. Whether caring for preschoolers or older children after school gets out, responding to the needs of older parents, or fitting in with a husband's work and vacation schedule, many women staff value having some flexibility in their work schedule to allow them to respond to these kinds of needs. When a church is able to provide the flexibility needed, the stress facing a woman associate staff member is reduced, helping her find more satisfaction and joy in fulfilling these diverse life roles. Even women whose children are grown value having flexibility in their schedule to spend time with their adult children and their grandchildren. The critical issues are to reduce the stress of conflicting demands and to maintain a balance in life among roles and responsibilities.

If you recognize that you face tension in fulfilling your roles in your family and at your church, you may want to explore with your supervisor or board ways that you can adjust your schedule to relieve some of that tension. Some possibilities include adjusting work hours to be home when your children are out of school, restricting the number of evenings you have to be out each week, doing some of your work from home, and having school holidays off. There may even be times when you would value a leave of absence (pregnancy or maternity leave, for example) or temporarily cutting the position back from full time to part time (for example, to care for an ailing parent or to accommodate a summer schedule when children are out of school) to free you to fulfill the family roles you value. Take the initiative to explore these kinds of possibilities to help you reduce stress and enjoy your ministry more.

Positive Feedback from the Congregation

One of the greatest sources of joy in ministry is felt when those with whom you minister affirm your ministry and gifts, demonstrate their support and belief in you, and let you know how much they appreciate your ministry. This topic is discussed more fully in chapter 3, but three aspects relevant to this discussion are highlighted here.

First, having those you minister directly with affirm your gifts for ministry is a powerful encouragement. This is especially true for those just starting out in vocational ministry. Before I could thrive in ministry

I needed to see that with God's help I was able to do the work I felt called to do. When you care deeply about your area of ministry and you want to serve God and the church to the best of your ability, the affirmation of your gifts for ministry is a powerful confirmation that you are where God wants you to be, doing what God wants you to do. It is easier to thrive, even in the face of problems and frustrations, when you have confirmation that your gifts and abilities fit well with the demands of your staff position.

Second, having the lay leaders of the congregation express their support for your ministry approach, for how you are going about it, is also very encouraging. This goes a step beyond affirming gifts for ministry to affirming you as a leader in ministry and your ministry strategy. This kind of support and encouragement is most evident when you are facing difficulties in ministry. Having lay leaders express confidence in how you are going about your ministry can be helpful when the immediate situation seems disappointing. Sometimes, when you're not sure that you are up to the demands of the situation, such support can help you see it through.

Finally, having others in the congregation express their appreciation for your ministry is also encouraging. Simple things like a word of thanks and a hug or a note in your mailbox can be a big boost to your spirits. This ministry of encouragement can be another confirmation that you are using your gifts in appropriate ways and that God is blessing your ministry. While God's affirmation of your work is most important, God uses members of the church to help. "Therefore encourage one another and build one another up, just as you are doing" (1 Thess. 5:11). This kind of encouragement can go a long way to help you persevere in ministry and find joy in what you do. One director of children's ministry expressed it this way: "I appreciate the support of my congregation. When someone says to you they appreciate you, they appreciate your ministry, they appreciate what you do with their children, that lets you know that you are valued!"

Taking Inventory: Questions for Reflection and Discussion

None of the environmental aspects described above is a must for thriving, nor will having all of these guarantee that an associate staff member will thrive in ministry. Each is part of a larger pool of factors that can enhance your ability to thrive. Ultimately, God is the one who works through the circumstances of our lives and ministries and can provide the grace to respond to the demands and difficulties we face. Part of how God does this is through the congregations we serve. As you consider looking for a church staff position or as you look at the congregational setting in which you currently serve, there are questions you may want to address as you consider how you can best thrive where God calls you. Many are asked in a yes-or-no format. You will have to determine which ones are especially important for you and whether any are aspects you feel provide an opportunity to work on to improve.

Ministry Candidates: Evaluating Prospective Ministry Settings

If you do not currently have a church staff position and are considering a ministry opportunity, or if you are in a position but are beginning to investigate other options, the following questions may be helpful as you prayerfully seek God's guidance.

A Healthy and Growing Congregation

1. Does the church have a sense of unity regarding its purpose and ministry vision?
2. Do you see an evident love for God and for others by church leaders?
3. Do people support the ministries of the church and actively help to achieve the church's ministry goals?
4. What recent history is there of how disagreements between church members have been handled? Is there good communication among the leaders even when they disagree on what the congregation should be doing?

Support for Your Ministry Area

1. Is support for this ministry area evident in the involvement and prayer support of the congregation?
2. Does the church fund this ministry area adequately to carry out the basic functions and activities that you think would be necessary? If not, have the church leaders expressed a willingness to do so?

3. Are opportunities in place to acquaint the congregation with this ministry area, helping them to see its value and be aware of ministry needs and accomplishments?

Openness to New Ideas and Approaches

1. Is the church asking you to come maintain a program, or is it open to your giving leadership in evaluating and strengthening what is being done?
2. As you talk with the staff and lay leaders of the church, do they seem open to looking at new ministry ideas?

Committed and Dependable Lay Leaders

1. Is there a history of rapid turnover of lay leaders in the major ministry areas of the church? In the ministry area you are interviewing for?

A Dynamic, Changing Position Description

1. Is the church open to annual evaluations of your ministry, the needs of the church, and possible adjustments to the position description if it is warranted?
2. How satisfied are you with the job description the way it is currently configured? If it were to stay the same for several years, do you think it would be a good fit for you?

Opportunity for Input into the Church's Broader Ministry

1. How important will it be for you to be involved in the broader ministry of the congregation beyond your specific job responsibilities?
2. Are sufficient opportunities present for you to interact on broader congregation issues at a board or staff level?

Opportunity to Focus on a Ministry Area of Passion

1. Given the range of ministry responsibilities in the staff position available, do you see sufficient opportunities to focus your

efforts on ministry areas you believe you are called to and gifted for?

2. Given what you understand of the position description, if you are concerned about this, can you negotiate this to some degree with the church leadership before accepting the position? Is there room to craft the position to more closely fit your areas of passion and preparation for ministry leadership?

Communication with a Supportive Church Board

1. Are opportunities present for the associate staff members of the congregation to interact with the congregation's governing board about their ministry areas?
2. Has the church considered assigning church board members to meet, talk, and pray with the church staff outside board meetings? If not, would they be open to looking at this option if you were to desire it?

Adequate Pay and Benefits to Provide for Family

1. Have you calculated the cost of living in the community your congregation serves? If not, can you get some help in developing a realistic family budget?
2. Does the congregation provide salary and benefits that would allow you to meet the needs of your family? If not, what other avenues are available to you to make up the difference (for example, your spouse also working; if the position is part time, finding an additional part-time job)?
3. As you consider the benefits offered, are they adequate to address your current and future needs (such as, health and life insurance, retirement benefits, tax status for housing benefit, ministry expense reimbursement allowance)?

Opportunities for Continuing Education

1. Does the church support its staff members' participation in continuing-education opportunities on a regular basis? Does it provide the funds and release time to allow staff to attend?

2. If the budget is tight and not much funding is available now, does the church support your developing inexpensive growth experiences, such as peer study groups, auditing a course at a seminary, or attending local ministry workshops?
3. At this point in your ministry, what kinds of continuing education would you benefit most from? Is the church willing to work toward allowing this to happen in the future?

Flexible Work Schedule to Address Family Needs

1. When the workload and time demands get especially heavy, does the congregation support its staff taking time off for personal rest and time with family?
2. Is there opportunity to adjust work schedules to allow for attending special family events and taking care of family needs as they arise? Is this an important issue to you, given your current family situation?

Positive Feedback from the Congregation

1. Do other staff members at the church report that they feel appreciated and supported by members of the congregation?

For Veterans: Building Support in Your Ministry Setting

If you are now serving on staff at a church and feel that one or more of the areas described in this chapter would benefit you but is not yet a strength of your congregation, here are some questions to consider that might help build greater support for you in your ministry. Focus on the ones that you think need to be addressed and find someone (supervisor, mentor, spouse, friend) with whom to discuss these questions and together determine what you can do to better address those that are having a negative impact on you.

A Healthy and Growing Congregation

1. How can you help reinforce the purpose and vision for ministry that your church leadership has for your congregation?

2. How can you voice support for the broad range of ministries of the congregation and not just your own ministry area? How can you encourage others to do the same?
3. If you are aware of tensions or disagreements with others regarding your ministry area, how can you work through them with those involved, listening to their concerns and affirming your commitment to unity in ministry together?
4. How can you affirm others for their ministries and help them rejoice in how God is working in your congregation? How can you express your appreciation for them and their ministries?

Support for Your Ministry Area

1. In what ways can you communicate with others in the congregation about your ministry area and efforts so they can know more about it, value it, and support it with their prayers? What misunderstandings do people have about your ministry area that you need to address?
2. If you feel that funding for your ministry area is inadequate, how can you present the goals, needs, and plans for ministry for the coming year and help the church leadership better understand the reasons for your budget requests? Is there more you can do to help them understand the value of what is being done and how the increased funding will benefit the congregation?

Openness to New Ideas and Approaches

1. If you feel that new ministry approaches are needed for your church to accomplish effectively the purposes of your ministry area, how can you begin to help others see the needs you see?
2. With whom should you discuss potential ministry changes? Who is in a position to help you understand how best to introduce the ideas you would like to see implemented?
3. Are you aware of the history of the current ministry approaches so that you understand why they are valued? If you would like to propose changes, how do your ideas fit with the priorities reflected in the current ministries?

Committed and Dependable Lay Leaders

1. Do you affirm others for their faithfulness in ministry and the importance of their work?
2. Does your church have in place means to supervise and support laypeople who take on ministry responsibilities? Is the turnover you experience due to inadequate support for them? What steps can you take or recommend to others that might improve lay leaders' experiences?

A Dynamic, Changing Position Description

1. Are you content with the present ministry responsibilities of your staff position?
2. If you would like to adjust your responsibilities, have you talked with your supervising pastor? What concerns do you think he or she might have? How could you respond to these concerns?
3. Is your church leadership open to conducting annual evaluations of staff and their ministry areas? If you would like to pursue this question, with whom should you talk?

Opportunity for Input into the Church's Broader Ministry

1. How can you take better advantage of any opportunities that already exist to have input into the broader ministries of the congregation beyond your own area of responsibility?
2. How can you encourage the church staff to take time to discuss your ministry areas with each other? Are you open to the input of others on staff about your own ministry area?

Opportunity to Focus on a Ministry Area of Passion

1. Are you content with the current distribution of workload you are carrying? Is it allowing you sufficient opportunities to focus on ministry areas you are most passionate about?
2. If your answer to the question above is no, who would you need to approach about reviewing your ministry responsibilities and

considering some restructuring to provide better focus to your work, reducing the stress or drain of diffused ministry efforts?

Communication with a Supportive Church Board

1. If you are able to attend church board meetings, do you go prepared with a report to share what is happening, what needs you have, and how others can support and pray for you and those you work with?
2. If you are not able to attend church board meetings, how can you provide a brief report that could be shared with them so that they are more aware of what you are doing and how they can support you?
3. Would your board be open to assigning board members to each staff member for encouragement, sharing concerns, and prayer support?

Adequate Pay and Benefits to Provide for Family

1. If you feel that your current salary and benefits are inadequate to meet your needs and those of your family, is there an appropriate person on the church staff or board with whom you can share your concerns?
2. Have you sought the help of a financial advisor in developing a personal or family budget and in financial planning for the future? What recommendations would your advisor make as to how the congregation could help you meet your needs (both salary and benefits)? How could this information best be shared with your church leadership?

Opportunities for Continuing Education

1. What opportunities for continuing education do you already have access to? Which ones that you have not tried might be of help to you?
2. How can you communicate the value of continuing-education opportunities to your supervising pastor and your church board? What specific goals could these opportunities help you achieve?

3. If congregation finances limit your options for continuing education, how might you take the initiative in developing some low-cost alternatives where you are? Who else might be interested in doing this with you?

Flexible Work Schedule to Address Family Needs

1. What are the heavy times of the year for your work schedule? How might you plan ahead and reserve some special times for personal renewal and with your family?
2. Can you discuss with your supervisor what latitude there might be in adjusting your work schedule to allow you to attend special family events and to care for family needs? What needs do you anticipate?
3. How can you assure your supervisor and other church leaders that you are adequately addressing the needs of your ministry area?

Positive Feedback from the Congregation

1. What kinds of feedback from the congregation are most meaningful to you? When you receive feedback, do you let others know that it encourages you?
2. If you feel that you are not getting much positive feedback from members of the congregation, have you mentioned this concern to your supervisor? He or she might be hearing some compliments about your work and be able to encourage others to pass them on directly to you.
3. Are there coworkers whom you can ask to give you feedback about your ministry, including both strengths and areas for growth, people who can help you see how God is using you to serve the church?

9

When You're Not Thriving

Why are you cast down, O my soul,
and why are you in turmoil within me?
Hope in God; for I shall again praise him,
my salvation.

—Psalm 42:5

By now you have become aware of a wide array of factors that characterize the thriving associate. And maybe you've experienced the rush of fulfilling and exciting ministry in your career path. But now ministry has become a chore, barely tolerable. Kevin and I feel your pain. We both have struggled in situations where the thrill was gone, the thriving only a memory.

My first "not thriving" experience happened while still in seminary. I was spiritually immature. The senior pastor with whom I served had a personality quite different from mine. Our ideas about what made good ministry did not align either. It was only a matter of time before these and other factors led to my resignation. Eight months—that was it. And I wondered if pastoral ministry was right for me at all. On a positive note, I did move on to another ministry that restored my enthusiasm for pastoral ministry. In addition, that seminary degree was earned, and upon graduation my wife and I were called to a pastorate in the Pacific Northwest.

After a decade serving as a senior pastor in this local church, my sense of thriving had ebbed. Pastoral ministry was still in my heart, but various ongoing frustrations were causing my soul to shrivel. What to do? Reflecting upon that season of life, my wife and I journeyed our way together, stumbling along as we watched God lead us faithfully to what has become a nearly thirty-year chapter of thriving service in seminary education. I would propose that those currently not thriving consider these three steps that we found helpful in our time of struggle.

Step 1: Consult Your Mentors

In chapter 6 we discovered that thriving associates herald the benefits of senior and peer mentors. One such associate put it this way:

> Find an older mentor and a peer mentor. Older because he [or] she will give you a broader perspective on ministry, life, and other areas. Peer because you guys are in similar positions in life and can be of good support to one another. Never go at ministry alone.

You may have some friends who will shoot the breeze with you, but mentors offer help others may not. Daniel Levinson, a psychologist who pioneered the field of adult development, defined a mentor as "ordinarily several years older, a person of greater experience and seniority in the world the young man is entering. . . . The term 'mentor' is generally used . . . to mean teacher, adviser or sponsor."[1] He suggests the effective mentor functions as

1. A teacher, enhancing the protégé's skill and intellectual development;
2. A sponsor, using his influence to facilitate the protégé's entry and advancement;
3. A host and guide, welcoming the protégé into and acquainting him or her with their new occupation, social world, values, customs, resources, and cast of characters;
4. An exemplar, modeling virtues, achievements, and a way of living;
5. A counselor, providing moral support to the protégé in time of stress; and
6. A supporter and facilitator of the realization of the protégé's aspirations. This is developmentally the most crucial role, according to Levinson.[2]

When we're not thriving we need mentors who exhibit such skills and commitments. One could say we all need a Barnabas who will guide us through the tough patches, much as that believer did for Saul of Tarsus, an apostle from whose thriving life and ministry so many benefitted. My wife and I have enjoyed such support throughout our forty years of serving in pastoral ministry in its varied forms. In our case supporters have included godly parents, "senior" friends, former local church pastors, along with several fellow associates and loving friends. God did not intend for us to struggle alone. Reach out and consult your mentors. And when you do so, a good place to start the conversation is with the factors that contribute to thriving and the related questions listed at the end of each chapter in this book.

Step 2: Seek Personal Counseling

I'll never forget that day when I was a parishioner in a large suburban congregation and the senior pastor casually referred to the therapy session he and his wife shared the week before. *Ministers can admit they are getting marriage counseling?* In one brief comment he normalized what some would consider taboo for spiritual leaders. My pastor revealed that every year he and his spouse went in for a marriage tune-up. It encouraged others to admit their need for help—and to seek it out.

Kevin and I would encourage you to take advantage of the resources offered by competent professional counselors. Our university has a school of psychology in which men and women are trained to help people to thrive in their life and calling. And while seeking a counselor may feel like a sign of weakness, thriving associate pastors are willing to face that perception and make the investment. As one simply shared with us, "Be teachable and always open to counsel."

While specialized counseling resources for ministers was less available years ago, these days there are numerous avenues through which one can get help. Aside from denominational resources, many retreat centers offer rest, relaxation, recreation, and professional counseling. Some centers are free to ministers, while others are quite costly. Yet more church leaders are investing in such support as they see the long-term benefit of being ministered to by staff members who are thriving in their service.

Freedom from reprisal is a huge concern in this endeavor, of course. There are settings in which seeking personal counsel is not supported and even used against us. Honesty and acceptance should be normative, but is often hard to find in organizational environments. You may find yourself breaking new ground and being a catalyst for change, as was the senior pastor I mentioned above. Living in misery and losing your joy of serving, however, is not worth playing it safe.

Step 3: Consider a Move

Let's face it. Sometimes we find ourselves in a situation that is not good for us or the people to whom we are seeking to minister. Again, Kevin and I have experienced this, as have many of you. While we believe that stepping out of full-time professional ministry for a season is sometimes healthy, we should also consider that our lack of thriving may indicate we need to move on to a new place or type of service.

I am often asked to help students and alumni discern whether or not they should make a ministry move. While the reasons for a change are usually complex, I suggest that they wrestle with six major areas of concern in contemplating a change.

Relational

Ministry is all about relationships. The extent to which we thrive depends upon their health. Knowing the hearts and minds of the people we have been called to serve is a prerequisite to faithful service. The extent of our personal concern for and investment in both congregants and fellow staff members will affect our sense of thriving, as will the depth of our personal walk with God. Moving on without addressing relational well-being is ill-advised.

Organizational

Thriving is very difficult if our personal sense of mission, vision, and values is not appreciated and supported by those we serve. In addition, ministry settings that do not provide the basic resources we need to carry out our calling make for frustrating circumstances. We need to know that in our contributing to any organization our presence is not harmful but beneficial to its overall mission.

Familial

Our family is what I like to refer to as our "first sheep." If a ministry setting is harmful to them, a move might be in order. On the other hand, staying might be the best thing, unless other circumstances (such as health issues, educational needs, or extended family concerns) necessitate a move. Regardless of these concerns, a sense of unity among family members is essential when considering a change in ministry setting.

Congregational

Congregations have seasons across their institutional life cycle. They can be emerging with springtime growth or settling into a winter cold spell. Sometimes we realize we don't fit a particular place because of where it is in its cycle of life. When I began my pastorate, the congregation was experiencing springtime. For a young, just-educated seminarian, the match was wonderful. But there might come a time when our gifts, skills, and aspirations do not fulfill the needs of a different season of a congregation's life. Such concerns need to be realistically addressed in considering a change of venue.

Emotional

Long-term depression, weariness, or other prolonged emotional struggles can signal a need for change. Unending criticism takes its toll on good and faithful servants. Personal feelings that one is not living up to his or her calling add to the mix of questions that can indicate a move to another place or even a time out for rest, retooling, and restoration. A new adventure, a place to start again and enjoy the invigorating experience of fresh winds and new vistas, can be just the right prescription toward restored health.

Professional

Before moving on, we must ask ourselves if we've given the present ministry our best shot. If not, maybe travel plans should be put on hold. Also, are we succumbing to the temptation of questionable values that can distort the integrity of our call? Bigger ministries aren't necessarily God's will, after all. However, you may have developed strengths and skills that are opening doors for new opportunities. And then the possibility exists that your present season of life and career is pulling you toward a different type of pastoral service or location.[3]

However one responds to the areas discussed above, thriving associate staff we know take their calling seriously. As one advised, "Be ready to die in your present ministry until God clearly tells you to move on." But when they contemplate a change, they make their moves carefully, being sure to cover such critical questions and considerations as they disengage and reengage through ministry transitions. Our hope is that regardless of your service setting, you will thrive as you navigate the realities of associate staff ministry.

Below are a series of questions related to the three actions suggested in this chapter. They are intended to encourage you to explore the reasons behind any lack of thriving you are presently experiencing and to help put you back on track for a new season of fulfilling and joyous service. Mentors who care about us want to help. Trained counselors have given their lives to assist us with tools to navigate this life successfully. Opportunities to serve are numerous, and making transitions to new and healthier places is possible. Each chapter in this book has described what thriving looks like and provides us all with a blueprint for building an effective associate staff ministry.

Taking Inventory: Questions for Reflection and Discussion

Consulting Your Mentors

1. Do you have a mentor? If so, when was the last time you spent some quality time with him or her? When could you reconnect and begin the process of working through your issues regarding this associate position, or ministry in general, and the challenges it presents?
2. Is there someone you've overlooked who could minister as a senior mentor to you? What must you do to connect with that person? Who are your peer mentors (see chapter 6) and which of these would be available to help you process the struggles you are currently having in your ministry?

3. If you have resisted finding mentors, are personal issues preventing you from seeking out such individuals?

4. Of all the issues mentioned in the chapters of this book, which are critical to your sense of not thriving and could serve as starting points for discussion with your mentors?

Seeking Personal Counsel

1. Related to question 3 above, are you willing to allow a counselor to help you discover any areas in your own life that may be preventing you from seeking a ministry mentor?

2. Are there resources available to you for personal counseling? Does your denomination offer such services? Are there contacts through your alma mater that could help you identify and cover professional counseling assistance?

3. Is your spouse willing to go to counseling with you? If you are single, is there someone who could partner with you as you seek encouragement and perspective regarding your ministry work and any personal issues related to your lack of thriving right now?

Considering a Move

1. Do you really know the people you work with and have a good understanding of how you fit into your present team? What kind of relational working environment do you need in order to thrive?

2. How are you doing spiritually? (See chapter 2.) Is your walk with God close, or have you neglected spending time in personal devotions? What steps might you take to ensure that your relationship with God is healthy and growing?

3. Knowing your own sense of mission and vision, is your present place of ministry a good fit? If not, is there hope that this might change, or should you pursue a more suitable ministry elsewhere?

4. In considering your immediate family members, would a change in your ministry location or vocation be advisable? How would a change help and harm them? Have you discussed such a change deeply and honestly with your spouse? If single, have you considered how a move would affect your social life, your friendships, and close family members?

5. Is your current ministry personally fulfilling and effective, or do you sense that your time and efforts here are coming to an end? Have you or this setting changed, so that a move might be advisable?

6. Are you emotionally ready to continue in this ministry, even though you're not currently thriving? Should you seek counsel (see above) to deal with this? Are other members of your family affected by your current situation to the point where they need counseling?

Part 4

Support from Church Leadership

Introduction

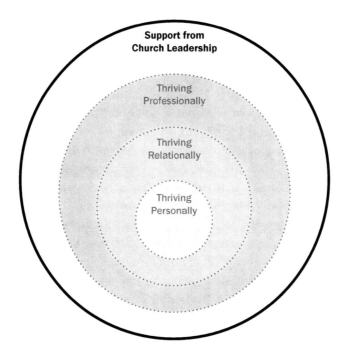

The chapters in this section are intended for those who supervise others on a church or parachurch ministry staff. The subjects of our research, thriving associate staff members representing many pastoral contexts, have illuminated our minds and hearts by describing the working environments that help them thrive. We have been on both sides of this equation, knowing the challenges of both leading followers and following the leader. While this book was written for associate staff, those who lead staff need to be aware of how they can contribute to the welfare of staff as they carry out their ministries. In chapters 10 and 11, we address this broader audience of supervisors and church boards. (Associate staff members may read this section themselves and then share it with the appropriate people in their ministry setting.)

For supervisors. As we listened to so many thriving associate staff, we realized we could pass on their collective wisdom to those who are responsible for their well-being. In chapter 10, supervisors will learn of twelve supportive strategies that will enable associate staff to thrive better and maybe even rise up to call them blessed! They will also discover additional practices that will equip and strengthen relationships among the staff. Whether a senior pastor, senior associate, or staff person responsible for overseeing others in ministry leadership roles, this chapter will give them many great ideas that are easy to implement and will help associate staff thrive.

For church boards. Chapter 11 is particularly directed to the men and women who serve on church boards or committees. Their support is crucial to the ongoing health and effectiveness of pastoral staff. We are aware that congregations of different denominations have various governance structures and processes, so we do not attempt to specify who needs to do what. Instead, we present issues and general principles to assist those who have the responsibility of overseeing the needs and work settings of associate staff members in their churches.

We encourage supervisors, associate staff, and lay leaders to read through chapters 10 and 11 and discuss them together. We hope that by doing so you will find increasing effectiveness and joy in ministry together. Working well as a team multiplies joys and relieves stress. May God enable you to experience that kind of relationship in your service with one another.

10

The Valued Ministry Supervisor

A senior pastor who believes in you, and loves you, is one of the most powerful influences in being able to thrive in ministry as an associate staff member. —A YOUTH PASTOR

Kevin and I (Mick) want to start by thanking you as a supervisor for your concern for the associate staff members with whom you serve. The fact that you are taking time to read this chapter shows that you care about them and their ministries. May God guide and bless you as you seek to be the kind of ministry supervisor who draws the best from associate staff members and helps them find deep satisfaction and joy in ministry.

Helping Associate Staff Thrive in Ministry

I am assuming you recognize how influential you are to your associate staff's sense of satisfaction and well-being in ministry. While it is true that each person is to carry out his or her ministry as unto God, not dependent on the praise of others, your leadership, example, encouragement, feedback, and support have a tremendous impact on your associates. You function as an overshepherd with those who labor with you. I have known such influence serving as a worship pastor, youth pastor, associate pastor, and senior pastor.

When long-term associate staff members were asked what helped them thrive in ministry, one of the first things mentioned was their relationship with you. Directly or indirectly, much of what influences their sense of satisfaction and well-being in ministry is touched somehow by you, their supervisor. When their work relationship with you is positive, they feel trusted, encouraged, supported, affirmed, and motivated for ministry. They feel that they are members of a team, partners with you in ministry, instead of ministry hirelings. They also feel that their ministry areas are valued, increasing congregational support. (For a fuller discussion of the benefits of a good work relationship between associate staff members and their supervisors, see chapter 5.)

Strengthening the work relationship between supervisor and associate staff member is an ongoing process that requires the thought and attention of both people. In chapter 5 we discussed issues that associate staff members need to address to meet the needs of their supervisors and to develop a positive relationship in ministry with you. Here we share what you can do to help your associates thrive in their ministries. We'll begin by looking at practices that thriving associate staff members value from their supervisors and then present a few specific things you can do that may help you respond to your associate's needs. Finally, the chapter closes with some questions for your reflection and for discussion with your associate staff.

What Associate Staff Value from Their Supervisors

Our research for this study (1997 and 2012) has consistently shown strong evidence of twelve ways of supporting your associate staff members that will endear you to them and facilitate their thriving in ministry.

Help Develop a Sense of Partnership in Ministry

Time and again, thriving associate staff members described working with their supervisor as a partnership in ministry or as serving together as a team. In our most recent study, 98 percent said that their supervisor treats them as a partner in ministry, not just an assistant, and that this attitude and treatment are very important to their longevity and satisfaction in ministry. This sense of partnership serves as a strong foundation for many of the other practices that will be described below. A basic attitude of acceptance and respect creates a climate for ministry that brings out the best in associate staff members and increases their satisfaction in ministry. Here are some ways this climate is developed.

Pay attention to labels and language. The titles that associate staff wear influence how people in the congregation perceive them and their work. The labels you use for your associate staff members communicate something of the value placed on them and their ministries and encourage the respect and support of the congregation. In addition, the language used by supervisors to talk about those they supervise communicates about their perceived status and value. More than the titles associate staff receive with the job, how you address them and how you talk about them to others can help create a team spirit and partnership in ministry together, or undermine it. Talking about "my staff" or "my assistants" does not communicate partnership in ministry; talking about "our ministry team" does.

Get to know and understand your colleagues in ministry. Taking time to get to know staff associates, their ministry gifts and passions, interests, personalities, and life experiences communicates that you value them and take their needs and ministries seriously. The better you know them, the better you will understand them and their motivations and goals for ministry. Taking time to really understand associate staff provides a platform for working well together and helps you work through those times of disappointment or conflict that can easily pull the partnership apart.

Respect the associate's ideas. Respect is a basic attitude toward a person that we communicate in many ways. One of the strongest ways to communicate this attitude to associates is to listen carefully to them and respond with encouragement to their opinions and ideas as you discuss ministry needs and opportunities together. Listening well communicates worth, even if you end up not using the ideas offered. When associate staff members feel that what they have to say is taken seriously, their sense of being part of a ministry team is built up.

Rejoice in the associate's success. One repeated theme that thriving associate staff members discussed was their supervisors' humble attitude and lack of a defensive ego. Their supervisors did not become jealous or envious of their success in ministry, but rejoiced with them when they did well or received praise from people in the congregation. Also, when supervisors received praise from the congregation for ministry successes, they made sure the congregation knew that the associate staff contributed to that success. This kind of support requires that a supervisor be secure in his or her own person and calling. Associates will sense this quiet confidence in you, which will help facilitate a cooperative team environment, instead of a competitive one where each seeks his or her own best interests.

Respond with mutual concern and aid. The quality of partnerships in ministry is best demonstrated in how we respond when a member of the team is hurt or struggling. In describing how the body of Christ is to function, Paul in 1 Corinthians 12:26 states, "If one member suffers, all suffer together; if one member is honored, all rejoice together." Demonstrating concern for each other and each other's ministries and assisting one another in times of need builds unity on a church staff and creates a sense of partnership in ministry.

Lead the Ministry Team with a Clear and Compelling Vision

While associate staff members want to be viewed and treated as colleagues in ministry, they do value and respect the leadership role of their supervisors. Supervisors have the responsibility of providing leadership to the congregation and to associate staff by helping to identify what they should be doing and how they should go about it. Associate staff members appreciate the supervisor who includes them in this process so that they too can embrace and own the vision for ministry. This inclusion helps them identify how their own areas of ministry relate to the larger picture. This shared vision-casting also makes developing ministry strategies, identifying staffing needs, and planning finances easier to accomplish. It is not always easy to do as you are swept along by your daily ministry demands, but regardless of the format, time needs to be *intentionally* set aside to accomplish this task. With this time investment, the staff develops a sense of being a team in ministry together, not just a collection of disjointed ministry specialists.

Before leaving this point, we would like to point out that frequently changing the vision is not conducive to the health and well-being of associates. I have had several former and present pastoral students relate how their senior pastor or other supervisor kept changing the vision of their congregation or mission. This usually leads to confusion, frustration, and a lack of cohesiveness within the team. Work hard together to develop the ministry vision, and then work long together to see it fulfilled.

Build Trust Together

Trust is developed over time and is frequently tested. When associate staff members were asked what their supervisors do that is important to their satisfaction and longevity in ministry, two items topped the list: they demonstrate trust and they believe in their associate's ministry abilities. Many study participants described trust as a two-way street that is strengthened over time as people handle their responsibilities and relationships well. Both parties need to make a commitment to work together toward the goal of building trust and to address promptly any problems that undermine it. Associate staff members describe three ways supervisors express trust and demonstrate that they themselves can be trusted:

They do not micromanage. Associates want to be able to do their work without their supervisor looking over their shoulder all the time. They want their supervisors to develop a trust in the associate's ability to be a self-starter, to work within the ministry guidelines that stem from the vision and purpose of the church, and to complete the work in a satisfactory manner. When associate staff members are fairly new, they may appreciate extra guidance and feedback, but once they have shown that they can handle their responsibilities, they need to feel trusted with them. Requiring regular progress reports is appropriate, as is offering encouragement and assistance when difficulties arise. Associate staff want to know that they can turn to the rest of the ministry team if they need help but that the responsibility still rests on their shoulders. One survey respondent commented:

> Either trust me or don't trust me. If you say you trust me but
> don't take any ideas seriously or let me know my ideas are
> good, then don't hire me. . . . I know you don't think you
> are a micromanager, but you probably are. If your staff meet-
> ing is longer than an hour, you are probably micromanaging
> each staff member. If you have a critique for each ministry/
> program/event, then you are micromanaging and eliminating
> trust and confidence in your staff. Let them do ministry (suc-
> ceed and fail) without offering advice (unless it is asked for).

They grant appropriate authority. Few things are more frustrating to associate staff than lacking the authority to do the jobs for which they are responsible. They greatly appreciate the supervisor who helps to identify what authority they need to do their work, and who then goes a step further to ensure that they have the ability to exercise that authority. To deny the associate the appropriate authority needed to do his or her work ensures frustration and failure. Delegating authority can be developmental, with a little authority being given to an inexperienced staff member and more given as experience is gained. The authority level should keep pace with the level of responsibility.

They allow the associate the freedom to fail and learn. Associates need to be able to try new ministry approaches and to learn through failure instead of having their judgment and ability continually questioned. How a supervisor responds to occasional failure communicates the level of confidence he or she has in the associate staff member. One associate pastor put it this way:

> If you give your staff responsibilities, also give them the mantle of authority to complete the tasks without your need to know and approve every detail. Allow them to complete the tasks, and trust that you have well placed your staff and they can do their job, and praise them highly and give them proper credit!

There will be aspects of their ministry that do not go well, but these are opportunities for growth. Debrief these experiences, but do so with grace and encouragement.

Be Available and Approachable

Associate staff really value being able to talk with their supervisors about ministry issues. Although they know you are busy with your own ministry demands, and they don't want to intrude when you need to focus on something else, your general availability is important. Ninety-seven percent of the thriving associate staff who participated in our 2012 study said that their supervisor's open-door policy with them enhanced their ministry satisfaction. They want to be able to discuss ministry problems and to troubleshoot with you. They respect your wisdom and experience and your knowledge of the congregation. They value your perspective on their work. There are also times when they will have ideas to share about areas of the church's ministry outside their area of responsibility. One associate suggested, "Walk around the office and get involved in the lives of the staff. Spend more time than you think you should every day talking with and listening to your staff. An hour a week with each member is the bare minimum. (Meetings don't count!)"

We know that supervising pastors are busy and need to establish boundaries to protect their own ability to fulfill their ministry responsibilities. Kevin's senior pastor had an open-door policy with the associate staff, but he also had two ways to protect his time. First, his open-door policy was literal: when his door was open, any of the staff could come in to talk. When the door was closed, it was because he needed time to work on something, and staff should wait to talk with him later. Second, the church secretary's office was right outside his, and he told her when he needed to be left undisturbed. She helped protect him from impromptu visitors, including those on staff.

One more thing needs to be said: Being available is not the same thing as being approachable. Associate staff need to feel that if and when they need to discuss something with you, you will listen to them and respect what they have to say. Proclaiming that your door is always open is not enough. If associates see you as defensive, argumentative, judgmental, or uncaring, they will hesitate to come to you for advice or help or to offer their ideas. If you're not sure how you come across to others, get some feedback from someone you respect, so that you can see if you are creating a work climate that encourages open communication with associate staff. And remember to focus on listening well to your associate. It's very easy to be thinking something else while pretending to listen. Even after forty years of marriage, I must work at giving my complete attention to my wife when we are in conversation. Setting aside issues at work and other distractions is crucial to being approachable.

Offer Support and Encouragement in Ministry

Support and encouragement need to be shown for associate staff members as well as their ministry areas. Some associates minister in ways that are readily seen and affirmed by the congregation. Others work behind the scenes and do not receive the same level of recognition and affirmation. The supervisor's public recognition and support for each team member, as well as that person's ministries, communicate the value of the ministry and the team member and greatly encourage those whose low-profile ministries do not receive as much spontaneous appreciation from the congregation. One staff associate, the only woman on her team, said of that public support and affirmation, "It makes me feel legitimate, like I'm part of this team. I'm not undervalued." One of our focus group members who served many years as an associate and now is a senior pastor commented, "Public support validates you in front of the whole church, when many in the congregation are not aware of or familiar with your contributions."

Some churches have established support teams to listen to and respond to staff members' personal needs, help troubleshoot problems they face, and encourage them in their ministries. Other things to consider in supporting associate staff members include giving them opportunities to be seen by the congregation in the worship service, providing them with public forums to promote their ministries, passing on other people's praise to them, and finding ways to educate the congregation about their work.

Care for the Person as well as the Ministry

Thriving associate staff members report that they feel genuinely loved and cared for by their supervisors. It is a matter of caring not only about their ministries but also for them as people. Showing interest in their personal and family life, encouraging them to take time away for spiritual renewal and strengthening family bonds, and taking time in meetings for sharing and praying about personal needs all communicate concern for them as individuals.

One practical way to care for associates is to allow a flexible work schedule so that they can adjust their time in the office according to the demands of evening meetings, weekend events, and family needs. Being able to take a morning off after a number of evenings out at meetings and having the freedom to attend a son's or a daughter's school event in the afternoon demonstrate the church's care for them as people.

Another way to care for associates is to be an advocate for them to the church governing boards regarding salaries and benefits. One major source of stress for associate staff members is the need to provide adequately for themselves and their families. As their supervisor, you have the opportunity and responsibility to bring their needs to the congregation and to see that they are adequately provided for. Although there are many ways of calculating compensation levels for associate staff members, one good benchmark is the salary and benefits that public-school teachers in your community with comparable education and experience receive. Keep in mind that schoolteachers work about a nine-month year compared to an associate staff member's twelve-month responsibility. Be sure to address health benefits and retirement pay as well as basic salary.

Demonstrate Loyalty

Associate staff members feel a great vote of confidence in their ministries when they know that their supervisors believe in them and will stand by them when others criticize. They need to know that someone is there to back them up when criticism comes. They are looking not for blind loyalty but for an expression of confidence in them that is not easily shaken. They want to know that when criticism is voiced, you will investigate it and listen to their perspective, rather than automatically siding with the person bringing the complaint. One female associate commented regarding a decision she had made and how poorly the senior pastor handled a criticism, "I felt unsupported in a decision I had made. I found out a congregant was talking to the pastor and he didn't take my side. It was about something really simple—and that kind of hurt. I thought he had my back."

Some associates value having their supervisors as a buffer, receiving the criticism and sorting it out with them. Others value having their supervisors refer all critics directly to them, not listening to the complaint until it has been brought directly to the associate staff member. Discuss this matter with your associates to determine how you will handle such criticism. The major issue is how you support associate staff members in the face of criticism, deferring judgment until you have a chance to talk the issue over with them. Another female associate shared a positive experience in this regard:

> A key thing for me has been a strong senior pastor who supported and protected me, was willing to stand up for me, and willing to take on people on my behalf. I was ordained at my church, which had never ordained a woman before. Until

years later I didn't realize that the pastor put his entire ministry, career, life, and reputation on the line for me. I'll tell you, that's an encouragement to stay in an associate ministry position when you have that kind of a senior pastor.

Keep Communication Open

Open communication is important to any team's ability to work well together, maintaining cooperative and unified ministry. Many excellent materials are available on improving communication, and the range of issues involved in keeping communication flowing well is enormous. Here we'll focus on a few issues for your reflection and further consideration.

First, associate staff members are greatly encouraged when you take the time and effort to listen to them even if you disagree with their ideas or perspectives. Most of us know what it is like to be asked for ideas in addressing a ministry need, only to have those ideas immediately shot down and our motives attacked. That experience makes us much more cautious and guarded in talking with that supervisor. We also know how motivating it is to have a supervisor actively draw out our thoughts and weigh them carefully, even if he or she has to disagree. That encourages our best efforts to think and share ideas.

Second, associate staff look to their supervisors to clarify ministry expectations and to help them respond to ministry opportunities and demands. Ongoing discussion is needed to clarify your expectations. Also, associate staff members may need your guidance on what they can do to work well with you and others on staff. What do you expect of them as you work together? What would help make your job as supervisor easier?

Third, associates appreciate supervisors who keep them informed of developments that have the potential to affect their ministry areas. Having the information necessary to make wise decisions and not being surprised by some announcement at a board or congregational meeting are important to their ministry satisfaction.

Fourth, associates appreciate supervisors who season their communication with a sense of humor. With so much stress in ministry, finding humor in the midst of ministry demands lightens the heart and helps keep discouragement at bay.

Fifth, associate staff members long for the ability to speak openly and honestly with their supervisors, sharing the ups and downs of ministry instead of constantly pretending to be on top of everything and in control. The ability to be open and authentic takes time to develop, but it will not happen without your example. With open communication, mutual support and prayer can be experienced at a deeper level, strengthening your commitment to each other's ministry success.

Finally, as disagreements or disappointments occur between staff members, associate staff value supervisors who do not allow these things to fester, disrupting the ability to communicate and work well together. As difficult as it may be, associates appreciate supervisors who address the conflicts or hurts and lead in the process of reconciliation. This action may take great measures of patience and grace, but the associate will have greater respect for you when the issues are resolved. When conflicts on staff are properly addressed, they can become an occasion for drawing you closer together.

Give Constructive Feedback

Associate staff members appreciate constructive feedback on their ministry efforts. Although none of us likes to hear criticism, receiving it and responding positively is easier when we trust the motives of our evaluator. Constructive feedback is critical to the ongoing growth and development of associate staff. Too many congregations do not have a good process in place to help the staff grow in effectiveness through evaluation. One of the most loving tasks you can undertake for associates is to develop and implement such a process. Here are a few guidelines:

First, give feedback on a regular basis, not just at an annual performance review. Part of your role as supervisor is to provide ongoing feedback to associates on what you believe is going well, their strengths in ministry, and areas for growth and improvement. Creating a culture of honest sharing, evaluation, and mutual support is conducive to thriving ministry.

Second, invite the associate's self-evaluation before providing your perspective. More often than not, associate staff members are aware of the problem areas in their ministries. If they bring it up, it will be easier for you to discuss it together and seek ways to help them through it.

Third, focus on associates' strengths, gifts, and ministry accomplishments first, then gently tackle one or two growth areas at a time. It's important that associates maintain hope in the process and perceive your positive regard for their ability. Focusing too much on what needs to improve can be discouraging, undermining the motivation and energy necessary to move forward.

Fourth, make sure that your feedback addresses their ministry efforts and strategies, not just the results. Circumstances outside their control may have influenced the final outcomes. Help them see the good in their efforts even if the outcome was less than what either of you had hoped for. If major problems need to be addressed, patiently walk with them through the process, even if it results in their eventual resignation from the church staff. Kevin shares this encouraging account:

> I will never forget working with one senior pastor as we met for weeks with a staff member I supervised, discussing our growing differences in ministry philosophy and the perceived problems in his ministry area. The senior pastor patiently listened to, encouraged, prayed with, and confronted the staff member over a few months. When the decision was reached that he should leave, it was a mutual one, and he was able to do so with the support of the church.

Be a Model and Mentor in Ministry

Associate staff members want to work with someone they can respect. It is far easier to receive direction and constructive feedback from a respected superior. Three key factors stand out in a supervisor that associate staff members feel they can respect.

First, associate staff are looking for a spiritual leader who will be an example to them. You don't need to try to appear perfect, because they value your honest sharing of spiritual struggles. They are looking for someone who has a heart after God and a commitment to carry out ministry in ways that honor God. They want a brother or sister in the Lord whom they can learn from, be encouraged by, and follow in ministry.

Second, they are looking for a person of integrity to follow, someone who is the same in public settings as in private meetings. They want to work under a person who strives to live by what she believes, who does not compromise personal commitments, and who is quick to repent and confess wrong attitudes or actions.

Third, they are looking for a person who is willing to learn and grow in ministry. This kind of positive model encourages them to want to grow and to be mentored by you and others. These three qualities encourage associate staff to give their best efforts to their ministries and to follow your leadership. One associate calls upon supervisors to model and mentor in this way:

> Love them, believe in them, inspire them, laugh (and cry) with them, show them how you're growing, and be an example for them. Do your best to be a follower of Christ and live a consistent life in the pulpit, in the office, and out in public, so that your associate can have someone to look up to.

Encourage Personal and Professional Development

More than 95 percent of thriving associate staff members in our more recent study described how their supervisors encourage them to keep learning and growing personally and professionally. This support and encouragement prevents them from stagnating and renews their energies for ministry. One thriving associate suggests to senior pastors and supervisors, "Help the staff to develop professionally. What helps their resume? Title bumps are free, and staff are less likely to look outside if they feel like they are moving forward at the church they are currently employed in."

Growth can be encouraged through a number of activities: retreats for spiritual growth and vitality; professional conferences for networking, encouragement, and skill development; continuing formal study in a degree program; marriage enrichment seminars; and other ministry workshops and continuing-education opportunities.

Two ways that you can encourage this ongoing development are to stir up the associate's desire to continue to grow and serve God more effectively and provide the opportunities to do so. Igniting an associate's desire to grow in ministry comes through your own example and your affirmation and active encouragement of his or her participation in growth activities. Providing the opportunities requires that the congregation make time available, provide financial support, and encourage the associate to find information about what is available. Work with your church board to develop policies that encourage the ongoing development of the staff by setting aside time and money for conferences and other continuing-education opportunities. These steps reflect the counsel of this associate: "Allow for budgeted items to include professional refresher courses, seminars, and conferences. Online is OK, but the need to be with others in the same field is imperative."

Encourage associates to identify the professional associations in their ministry areas and other formal and informal educational opportunities from which they can benefit. Don't forget to look for personal enrichment opportunities that can renew them and facilitate growth. Make sure these kinds of enrichment activities are acceptable for receiving financial support from the church budget.

Pray for and with Them

We began this section by focusing on the foundational need to develop a sense of partnership in ministry, and now we close it with another foundational issue, your prayer support for associate staff. This attention to prayer is not lip service to what we think is spiritually correct but a recognition of a vital part of healthy multiple-staff ministry that influences many other areas. Even as Kevin and I have worked on this project, a group of our fellow faculty associates have supported us in prayer. Every week they gather to pray for many needs and issues. And every week they ask how things are going with our endeavor. Knowing that others are walking with us and regularly praying for us has served as a comfort and encouragement throughout the course of this research and writing.

If you supervise female staff, you should know that our research shows having one or more prayer partners has a significant impact on female staff members' ability to thrive in ministry, even more so than for men. Both value it highly, but women associate staff members score this higher in impact than do the men. Because of the stresses and challenges of ministry, it is important that female associates have people they can turn to who will pray for them, asking that God would give them wisdom, grace, and strength to carry out their ministry. Women associate staff members rate prayer partners as a very strong influence on their ability to thrive. These partners can be members of a support or accountability group, members of the congregation, or members of one's immediate family. In fact, in many cases it is other women in the congregation whom the woman staff member looks up to as people of spiritual maturity. Some women find it beneficial to have one or two close prayer partners with whom they share deeply and many others who help pray for their ministry needs in more general ways. Supportive supervisors help their associates identify people who can intercede for them and their ministry.

Whatever else you do in response to the items discussed above, commit yourself to pray for and with associate staff. *Pray for them,* and tell them you are praying for them. Find out what they would like you to pray for and do so. Ask them to share how God answers those prayers and rejoice with them. *Pray with them,* and let them pray for you. Take time during the week to share together and pray together for each other, your ministries, and the needs of the church. *Pray in public* for your associates. Lift up them and their ministries and encourage others to pray for them as well. *Pray in private* for your associates, asking God to strengthen, guide, protect, and bless them as they serve in the church. Enlist others to pray for them, so that each staff member knows that there are people in the congregation to whom they can turn for prayer support.

Practices That Strengthen Staff Relationships

As we interacted with veteran associate staff members who were thriving in ministry, we asked them what specific practices supervising pastors did that helped them thrive in ministry. Here are a few that we heard most consistently.

Hold Regular Staff Meetings

Because of the importance of open, ongoing communication, the need to develop a united team effort in ministry, and the power of mutual encouragement and prayer, regular staff meetings can be one of the best investments of your time with associate staff. Carving out time in the schedule to meet weekly and making it a priority for all staff members help foster a sense of being part of a ministry team. Most of you probably already have regular meetings with your associates. Let us recommend five things you can do in your staff meetings that can be of great benefit to you and associate staff.

Refocus the vision. The daily demands of ministry can blur your staff's vision of what they are striving for. Take time together to renew your vision of what God has called the congregation and its staff to be and do. This vision refresher can increase motivation for ministry. It will also help your focus in the rest of your meeting as you review ministry efforts and needs and determine what should be done next.

Debrief ministry efforts, needs, and new goals. With each staff member working in different ministry areas, take time to allow each person to report on what's been happening, what successes and difficulties they are facing, and what needs and goals they are addressing. This means that the agenda for your staff meetings is created by all the staff, not just you. As each person contributes to the staff meeting, ownership of the meeting and interest in each other's ministries grow.

Troubleshoot together. As difficulties are raised by various staff members, determine which issues should be tackled by the group together and which should be dealt with in some other setting. One benefit of troubleshooting ministry problems together is the development of mutual concern and care for each other and for each other's ministries. Later, as good things happen in those ministry areas, the whole staff rejoices. Your staff members have much wisdom that each member can benefit from. Encouraging them to assist each other builds their unity and commitment to each other. And as is true in all staff interactions, do this in a safe atmosphere of mutual respect, confidentiality, and trust.

Learn together. A staff benefits from studying and learning together. Taking time for this activity may seem an impossibility with everything else that needs to be done, but the benefits can be tremendous. Take time to study Scripture together, and relate it to personal or ministry concerns. Building a strong biblical foundation for life and ministry can influence a lifetime of ministry. Taking time to read and study relevant books that deal with societal needs or ministry approaches can challenge your ministry team to consider how better to minister in your community. Studying together allows you to build common ground in your convictions, ministry philosophies, and goals. This strengthens your unity in ministry and focuses your efforts on common ends. It is a worthwhile investment of your time.

Pray together. Whatever else you do, don't neglect this important aspect of meeting together. Staff members need to know that they are supported in prayer, both in their ministry responsibilities and in their personal needs. Staff meetings that focus on reporting, planning, and troubleshooting but neglect prayer can be draining and discouraging. Take time to pray together for your staff's needs and those of the church. If your staff is large, consider varying how you do this, praying together sometimes and praying in pairs at other times. Over time, this practice will allow you to pray individually with each staff member. Believe us, this can mean a lot to associates and to your growing unity as a ministry team. Finally, as you see prayers answered, take time to revisit them and give thanks and praise to God together. Reviewing how God has worked and worshiping together strengthen faith and hope for times when difficulties arise.

Conduct Staff and Personal Retreats

All ministry positions have their share of stresses and problems. As you and your associates carry out your ministries, it is easy to become worn out, drained by the constant demands of the job. Your spiritual vitality can suffer periods of dryness or a sense of becoming routine. Having times to retreat for renewal and growth can help a staff member thrive in ministry over the long haul. Carving out time for this can seem nearly impossible, but it needs to become a priority to help everyone remain spiritually healthy and effective in ministry. Stephen Covey likens taking time for personal renewal to sharpening a saw.[1] You can cut more wood, with less work, with a sharp saw than you can with a dull one. The time invested sharpening the saw is worth the effort. Consider ways you can help associate staff with their personal spiritual renewal through retreat opportunities. A few beneficial types of retreats and breaks for personal renewal are described below.

Staff retreats. Taking time away together as a staff can help build friendships and mutual support for each other. Some retreats can focus on vision and goals for ministry and on building unity. Others can focus more on personal spiritual health and growth, allowing you to support each other in keeping your relationship with God vital and taking steps toward greater spiritual maturity. Whatever focus your retreat has, make sure there is time together for fun and relationship building. Don't turn it into one long staff meeting. If time and money for a staff retreat are not already available to you, you may need to discuss this plan with your church board, helping board members to see the potential benefits for your staff's effectiveness in ministry.

Personal retreats. Providing opportunities for associates to take time away for personal retreats can boost their spiritual vitality. While extended time away (a few days) can be helpful, even a day or less away to read Scripture, pray, and be in fellowship with God can be renewing to the spirit. Consider developing a policy that allows staff members to take time for personal retreats, and check within your congregation and denomination to identify free or inexpensive places where staff members could go for a day or an overnight. Lead by example in this area, and share how it benefits you. Your example can encourage associates to take time for a retreat as well.

Sabbaticals. People in all kinds of ministries are seeing the value of providing their staff with sabbatical breaks. These usually come after some years of service, varying in length based on the time served in one's position. We are hearing of three-month sabbaticals for staff who have served three to four years. The associate is expected to get some rest, perhaps explore a new idea for or read up on their ministry area, and just decompress from the relentlessly exhilarating world of pastoral service. Kevin and I enjoy this feature in the world of academia and think it should be a more regular feature in all ministry settings.

Take Time to Socialize Together

Associate staff members value the opportunity to get to know their supervisor and a supervisor's effort to get to know them. When church staffs take time to know each other, they build bridges that encourage open communication, mutual understanding, and mutual acceptance. Having occasional meals together, taking time in staff meetings for personal sharing and prayer, throwing birthday parties, and sharing recreational activities together all provide opportunities to get to know each other better and foster a supportive fellowship in ministry.

You don't have to be best friends, and you don't have to share the same hobbies to build positive relationships that help you work well together. Kevin remembers one supervisor he worked with:

> One of my senior pastors was a marvelous example in this regard. We took time in our staff meetings for personal sharing as well as church ministry issues. He hosted Christmas dinners and summer cookouts for the staff and their spouses. These casual times and special events helped us all know each other better. We became friends and respected each other in ministry, despite our many differences. These activities went a long way to help us work through conflicts that arose in our ministry together.

Hold Celebrations

Kevin is a big fan of celebrations by people who are working together in ministry. While my experience is limited in this area, Kevin has convinced me of its power in supporting associate staff. So, let's listen to his wisdom and counsel.

> I have to confess, this last recommendation does not come directly from this study of thriving associate staff members, but from my own observations and convictions about encouraging people in ministry. Two aspects of congregational ministry can undermine a person's motivation and sense of accomplishment. First, much of what we are seeking to accomplish is hard to measure and develops over long periods. Progress is hard to identify at times, and maintaining energy for ministry when we cannot see clear results can be difficult. Second, the daily demands of ministry can keep us so busy that we do not take time to reflect on the good things that have been accomplished. We're so busy "doing the ministry" that we do not take time to rejoice over what God has done in and through the church. These two things can dull one's ability to find joy in ministry. Allow me to propose a simple remedy.
>
> I have become a great believer in the power of celebrations. Just as the nation of Israel used festivals to remember

what God had done and to give praise for divine love and mercy, we who serve on church staffs need times to recognize what God has done and to give praise for it. What the church and church staff need is more celebrations! For example, dinner together to celebrate the launch of a new ministry effort, eggnog and cookies together after a meaningful choir concert, or a time of prayer and singing together as you reflect on the ministries of various laypeople in the church are all simple ways of celebrating God's work in your church.

We will find much to be thankful for if we look around us and see how God is working in our congregations and communities. There is much to celebrate as associate staff members pour their energies into their ministry areas–people coming to faith in Christ, people moving forward in discipleship, new people coming to the church, big events going well, volunteers being recruited and equipped for ministry, financial resources being given to support ministry efforts, people worshiping the Lord. It's too easy to keep our focus on our never-ending needs in ministry and neglect to rejoice as God provides for us and works in our midst. As a supervisor, consider how you can celebrate with your associates what God is doing.

All the practices discussed above are ways to strengthen your work relationships with each other as partners in ministry. They are well worth the intentional effort required to plan them and carry them out. They are an investment that pays off in reducing conflicts, providing encouragement, and building support for each other's ministries.

Taking Inventory: Questions for Reflection and Discussion

Some of the questions that follow may be good for you to reflect on privately; others may be good to discuss with your associates. Your ministry situation is unique, and these questions may trigger other issues that would be more helpful for you to consider. Use these questions in ways that will be of the most assistance to you and to your associates. (Additional questions to consider for discussion with your associates can be found at the end of chapter 5.)

Developing a Sense of Partnership in Ministry

1. How do you view those you supervise in ministry? If it is hard to feel that they are really partners in ministry, what do you think is preventing that sense of partnership from developing?
2. Do their titles encourage congregational support and respect for them and their ministries?
3. Does the language you use convey to them and to others a sense that you view them as part of a ministry team?
4. How well have you gotten to know your staff as people? What things could you do together to get to know each other better?
5. In what ways is your respect for associate staff expressed? Are there things you do that might communicate a lack of respect for staff or their ideas?
6. How do you find yourself reacting when people praise associate staff? Is your reaction something you need to seek God's help to correct?

Building a Clear and Compelling Vision

1. Have you clearly articulated together your understanding of God's purpose and vision for your congregation? Have you discussed this with your associates and taken time to help them identify how their ministries tie into and support the larger vision for the church's ministry?
2. Are you setting time aside on a regular schedule to revisit your congregation's vision for ministry and use it to help focus your ministry efforts?

Building Trust Together

1. How are you feeling right now about the trustworthiness of your associate staff? What issues would need to be addressed before your trust in them could be strong?
2. As you think over the last few months or years, is there anything that you have done that might be hindering your associates' ability to trust you as their supervisor? What steps could you take to restore that trust?

3. Do you find yourself checking up on associates' work a lot? Why do you think you do this? If the congregation's associate staff need to gain ministry experience and skill, how can you help them work toward more independence in their work?

4. How do you react when associates fail in some aspect of their ministries? How could you help them deal with their own sense of failure and learn from these experiences?

Being Available and Approachable

1. How available are you to associate staff? In what ways can you communicate your desire to be available to them when needed, but also protect the time you need to fulfill your own ministry responsibilities?

2. Do you have a sense of how approachable you are as a person? How do you deal with criticism or complaints from others?

3. Is there anything you can do to communicate better your desire to have associates share freely with you their ideas, concerns, and frustrations?

Offering Support and Encouragement in Ministry

1. Do you have a sense of how much encouragement associate staff members receive from others in the church? If you suspect that they may need more, how might you go about providing it?

2. Are there regular opportunities for the congregation to see and hear from associate staff regarding their areas of ministry?

3. Do you publicly talk about associate staff and their ministries, encouraging others to pray for them and support their efforts?

4. Would associate staff members appreciate having a lay-support team meet with them to encourage them and address their needs in ministry?

Caring for the Person as well as the Ministry

1. Do you find yourself occupied primarily with how well associates' ministries are going and not paying much attention to how associates are doing personally?

2. Are there regular times when you and your associates share and pray together for both ministry and personal needs?
3. In what ways are you communicating to associates how important they are to you and your concern for their well-being?
4. Is there flexibility in associates' schedules to allow them to have time with their families, especially when evening and weekend ministry demands are heavy?
5. Are you an advocate to the church governing board to provide a fair salary and benefit package for associate staff?

Demonstrating Loyalty

1. How have you responded when someone has come to you with criticism of your associates? Did your response demonstrate loyalty to your associates and concern for them?
2. Would your associates prefer to have people come directly to them with criticisms or come to you first as their supervisor?

Keeping Communication Open

1. Does how you listen demonstrate that you are genuinely interested in your associates' ideas, opinions, and insights?
2. Are you clear in communicating your expectations of associate staff members?
3. Do you keep associates informed of matters that have the potential to affect their ministry areas?
4. Do you find yourself being intense and serious all the time with your associates, or do you find ways to allow humor to lighten the work atmosphere?
5. What level of transparency characterizes how you and your associates talk with each other? Would your ability to work well together be enhanced by greater authenticity than what you have now? How might you begin moving in that direction?
6. How do you tend to deal with conflicts and hurts with your associates? Are there any unresolved hurts that need to be addressed for reconciliation? What do you fear might happen if you try to resolve this now?

Giving Constructive Feedback

1. Do you have a process in place to help associates evaluate their own ministries and receive constructive feedback from you?
2. Is evaluation a regular part of your work together with your associates?
3. When you have conducted evaluations, have you focused primarily on associates' strengths and successes in ministry, helping them identify and work on one or two growth areas at a time?

Being a Model and Mentor in Ministry

1. Are you comfortable with the idea that associate staff members look to you to be an example to them in spiritual growth, ministry integrity, and openness to learn? Is there anything that you fear will cause them to lose respect for you as their leader? What steps can you take to address this concern?

Encouraging Personal and Professional Development

1. Do you encourage associates to take advantage of continuing-education opportunities regularly, to participate in professional organizations, and to benefit from personal growth opportunities?
2. Does your congregation provide staff with time and money to do the kinds of things listed in the previous question? If not, what steps could you take to encourage the church to do more in this area?

Praying for and with Them

1. Do you regularly pray for and with associate staff members? Do you pray for both their ministry and their personal needs? Do you let them know that you are praying for them?
2. Do you encourage others in your church to pray for your associate staff members as well?

3. Are there ways you could help your staff identify prayer partners, given their areas of ministry and gender?

Holding Regular Staff Meetings and Retreats

1. Do you meet weekly as a staff to refocus your vision for ministry; debrief your ministry efforts, needs, and goals; troubleshoot ministry problems together; pray together; and learn together? Which of these areas are your strengths, and which ones should you take more time to do together?
2. Have you ever had a retreat together as a staff? If so, how did it benefit you? If not, how might this kind of experience benefit you as a ministry team? Where could you go that would not be too expensive? How can you carve out time for a retreat?
3. Can you provide opportunities for the church staff to take personal retreats once or more a year? Again, how can you get the congregation to provide the time and money? What resources do you have nearby to take advantage of?
4. Could you explore the idea of sabbatical leaves for associates? What are other churches and ministries doing to provide this kind of support?

Taking Time to Socialize Together and Holding Celebrations

1. Do you as a staff take time for socializing, enjoying time together away from the church office? What mutual interests do you have that you might pursue together? How can you be sensitive if in your staff situation all members except one are the same gender?
2. What kinds of events (holidays, birthdays, sporting events) might you use as excuses to get together and have a good time with your families? Will these events be comfortable for your staff who are unmarried?
3. Do you take time as a staff to reflect on what God has done in your church and to celebrate it together? How could you make this a regular part of your staff meetings?

Fostering Feedback to and from Your Associates

Here are a number of questions that you may want to discuss with associate staff members. You may learn a lot just by taking the time to listen to their responses and encouraging them to ask further questions for your response.

1. What three to five things could you do as their supervisor that would help them as they carry out their ministry responsibilities?
2. Share with associates the three to five things they could do that would help you most as their supervisor. Why are these important to you? How do they feel about these things?
3. When you have disagreements about ministry issues, how do you want to deal with them to best work through them?
4. What things could you do that would help in building a cooperative ministry together?
5. Are there any areas where one or the other of you has felt that trust or loyalty in your work relationship has been compromised? Has anything taken place that has caused your respect for each other to suffer? If so, what can you do to resolve the problem?

11

The Supportive Church Board

*A few of the kids in our youth group were going through some really
tough times, and one of the elders came to me and said, "Let me know
if there is anything I can do to help. I've got your back covered." That
kind of support from the church means a lot!* —A YOUTH PASTOR

After serving as an associate staff member in churches for eleven
years, I (Kevin) moved into teaching Christian education at a seminary in Canada. While my family and I were there, I had to adjust
to no longer being a church staff member. That was a growing experience for me, as I gained a new perspective on being a part of
the body of Christ and an appreciation of the pressures of being an
active layman in the church. After two years of volunteer service in
the congregation's educational ministries, I became an elder, serving
on the governing board of the church. It was quite a challenge as we
sought to work with and support our pastoral staff and together guide
the church in its ministries. One concern I developed during that time
was about how we as the church governing board could support and
encourage our associate staff members. We were so used to working
with the senior pastor that we did not often spend much time considering the needs of other staff members. It is unfortunate that this pattern seems to be all too typical.

Now, many years after the first edition of this book came out, I
am again serving on the governing board of my congregation, and I
again am aware that we have a responsibility for the supervision and
support of the entire vocational ministry staff, not just the senior pastor. Like you, I wonder, what is our role in helping our church staff do
well in their ministries and thrive in the process?

In most churches, the supervision and support of associate staff rest
entirely in the hands of the senior pastor. While your senior pastor or

other associate staff supervisor has the most direct responsibility for supervising and supporting the associate staff, there are things that lay leaders can also do to enhance their associate staff's ministry experience and effectiveness.

This chapter is written for those who, like me, serve as lay leaders in their church governing structure. In some congregations, this may be an elder board, while others have sessions, administrative boards, church councils, or deacon boards. Whatever your church's structure, if you have responsibility to oversee ministry and personnel, this material is for you. Throughout, I will use the term *board* to describe your group.

I want to suggest ways that you and your board can support your congregation's associate staff members, helping them to serve with deep satisfaction. By supporting them, encouraging them, stretching them, and caring for them, you can invest in their ministry and help them thrive where God has placed them.

These insights emerged from two studies (1996–97 and 2012) of long-term associate staff members who are thriving in their ministries. Through focus-group discussions and a survey of veteran associate staff members in more than fourteen denominations in the United States and Canada, we have gained an inside look at what contributes to their satisfaction, personal well-being, and longevity in ministry. (Details of the study are summarized in appendix A of the book.) Approximately six hundred survey respondents have described what their supervisors and church boards can do to help them thrive in ministry. Their responses have been grouped and summarized below, with questions for your reflection and discussion provided at the conclusion.

Thank you for caring enough about your church staff to read and act on these suggestions. May God guide you as you carry out your important role of leadership in your congregation and as you support and care for those who serve with you.

Create a Supportive Ministry Environment

It is important to understand how great an impact the working environment can have on workers' motivation, effort, and satisfaction with their work. I'm sure you know that when people feel supported and respected, and when they are provided with the resources needed to get their work done, they feel energized and motivated to do it well, even in the face of significant challenges and problems. When the work setting is characterized by a lack of unity, support, and respect, motivation is hard to maintain and discouragement can easily set in. Your church's associate staff members will face many challenges in their ministries; at times they will feel discouraged and wonder if they are doing the right thing by serving here. The ministry environment that you and their direct ministry supervisor help create can make a big difference in their ability to persevere through the challenges, see God at work, and find deep satisfaction in their own work. Here are some specific things that you and your church board can do to help.

Focus on Keeping the Church Healthy

The general relational health of your congregation has a great impact on all your staff members as they carry out their ministries. A church with unity of ministry vision, where church members understand the importance of finding ways to use their gifts in the body, where political maneuvering is discouraged, and where people are able to work through hurts and disagreements and to keep bitterness from gaining a foothold—that is the kind of environment that allows your staff members to focus their attention and energies on their ministry responsibilities. By maintaining the relational health of the congregation, your board is providing a supportive environment for your pastor and associate staff. Make sure that with all the major initiatives, decisions, and projects your board addresses, you do not lose sight of the need to promote the health of your congregation as members relate and work together in ministry. Everything you do in this area benefits both your congregation and your staff. It also honors God.

Affirm and Encourage Your Staff

When veteran associate staff members described what helped them thrive in ministry, near the top of the list was that the church's lay leaders supported and believed in them and affirmed their gifts for ministry. They also benefited greatly from receiving words or notes of appreciation and encouragement from those to whom they ministered. With the frequent stresses of their ministries and the fact that much of what they do may be carried out behind the scenes, your verbal affirmation and encouragement can be a powerful boost to how they feel about themselves and their ministries. Paul tells us to "therefore encourage one another and build one another up" (1 Thess. 5:11). Your board can have a ministry of encouragement to associate staff. When you tell them that you believe in them, respect them, support them, recognize their gifts, and appreciate their ministries, you encourage their hearts. While God's ultimate affirmation of them is of utmost importance, God can use you to help them see how important they are to your church. You can be that means of grace that lifts them up when needed.

Build Support in the Congregation

When associate staff members feel that their congregations value and support them and their ministry efforts, it boosts their motivation to do their best. Strong congregational support for associate staff can be built in many ways. Look over the suggestions that follow, and see which ones are possible in your congregation.

Attend to titles and ordination or licensing. The title and ordination or licensing status that associate staff members carry can influence how congregation members view and respond to them. In our culture, titles communicate something about the status of people and their work. Titles such as *pastor* or *minister* imply greater status than *director* or *leader.* In addition, staff members who are ordained or licensed by their church or denomination may be viewed with a level of respect not given to nonordained or nonlicensed staff. The goal here is for church leaders to encourage congregation members to respect, value, and support those who serve on the church staff. Using titles that encourage respect can help your staff. Recognizing ministry calling, preparation, and gifts through ordination or licensing can also promote congregational support for your associates. Some denominations have guidelines on titles or ordination tied to educational preparation, type of ministry responsibilities, gender, and confirmation of gifts and calling. Take a look at what your church is able to do, and find ways to promote respect for your associates and their ministries in the congregation. Even if ordination or licensing is not possible, a congregational commissioning service can help build support for your associate staff members in their ministries.

Ensure visibility. Provide opportunities for associate staff to be seen and heard by the congregation. For some associate staff, such as a minister of music, visibility happens naturally every week. For others, such as a youth pastor or children's pastor, visibility may take more intentional planning. Public recognition and support for your associates grow with public exposure. For churches with large associate staffs, this may mean developing a schedule for them to take turns helping with some aspect of public worship. However you do it, find ways for your congregation to see and hear from its associate staff on a regular basis.

Educate the congregation. Find ways to educate the congregation about what associate staff members do and its importance. While you may have a good understanding of what staff members do in their ministries, many in the congregation may not. It is often a mystery, especially if the associate's work is behind the scenes rather than up-front on Sunday morning. When your congregation understands and values the work your associate staff does, a sense of support grows that your associates can feel. Highlighting their ministries in the church newsletter is one way to keep the congregation informed and to build support for associate staff.

Encourage affirmation. As people get to know more of what the associate staff members do, encourage congregation members to share words or notes of appreciation with them. Receiving this affirmation from those whom they labor to serve on God's behalf means a lot to associate staff. Taking time in public gatherings to recognize and affirm the ministries of associate staff is a good way to prime the pump of encouragement.

Provide Needed Ministry Resources

A congregation that provides associate staff members with the authority and resources needed to carry out their ministries demonstrates a high level of respect for them as ministers and for their work. Conversely, when a staff member is given a ministry responsibility but lacks the resources to do it well, mixed signals are sent about the importance of that ministry to the church. Your church board has the responsibility of making sure that the church staff has what is needed to fulfill ministry responsibilities. Take a look at your budget and what it communicates to your associate staff members. Do they have what they need to do the job? If not, what can be done to address this?

Connect and Have Fellowship

Take time to get to know your church's associate staff members. It's easy for church board members to focus on getting to know the senior pastor, but the associate staff can benefit from your personal interest and encouragement as well. Take time to know them as people, not only as staff members. Consider pairing up with another lay leader and take an associate staff member out for coffee, and enjoy the time getting to know them. Help them and their families to feel loved and appreciated for who they are, not just for what they do for the church. Help them feel they are a part of the church body, not only employees. This effort will go a long way toward building a team spirit and making their ministry with you a source of satisfaction.

Provide Prayer Support

For those on your staff, knowing that you, as the lay leaders of the church, are supporting their ministry efforts and personal needs in prayer is a great encouragement. Take time in your meetings to pray for and with them. Make this a regular part of your agenda. As individual board members, pray for them during the week on a regular basis. Take time to talk with them outside your meetings and ask how you can support them in prayer. Occasionally take time with them individually to pray for them and their ministries. Prayer builds a sense of partnership in ministry and encourages the heart. It is a means by which God allows us to join in the task of meeting the needs of others. Make this a priority for supporting your associate staff.

Encourage Associate Staff to Lead

Providing a supportive environment is an important beginning, but how you actually work with and respond to your church's associate staff members as they carry out their ministries can contribute to their satisfaction or discouragement. Here are three ways that you can encourage associate staff to exercise proper leadership in their ministries and find satisfaction in the process.

Clarify Job Description and Expectations

The senior pastor or other staff supervisor may take the lead in clarifying the roles of associate staff members, but it is important that you as a board and the associate staff members are on the same page regarding their ministry responsibilities and the church's expectations of them as staff members. A common understanding reduces conflicts, helping staff members know when they can exercise authority and when they need to seek approval to act from their ministry supervisor or the board. Misunderstandings in these areas create headaches, frustration, and discouragement. Preventing miscommunication is a worthwhile investment of time and effort. At least once a year, take time at your board meetings to review each staff member's responsibilities and how you expect them to be carried out. Also, review your responsibilities toward staff and what staff members should be able to expect from you.

Be Open to New Ideas and Risk Taking

Associate staff members appreciate ministry supervisors and church boards that trust them enough to let them try out new ministry approaches. They want to be able to explore ways to make their ministries more effective, not just maintain the status quo. This experimentation requires that church leaders grant them some opportunity to take initiative and the freedom to take risks. While this freedom may need to be earned over time, as associate staff members mature in their ministries they need to feel that they are trusted to exercise more authority in initiating changes in how their ministries are carried out. Some ideas will meet with success, others will not. For associate staff members to thrive in their ministries, they have to be able to take some risks without feeling that their job is on the line every time something doesn't go right. A degree of freedom to try and to fail encourages initiative and creativity, opening the way toward increased ministry effectiveness.

Invite Input into the Broader Ministry of the Church

As time goes on and associate staff members gain ministry experience and knowledge of the congregation and community, they appreciate church leaders' inviting and listening to their input on ministry issues outside their direct area of responsibility. Being invited to do so is a vote of confidence in them as church leaders whose insights and perspectives are respected. Many such opportunities will occur in church staff meetings as the staff discusses ministry needs. However, this interchange can also be encouraged by allowing the associate staff to participate to some degree in the meetings of the church board. Some congregations include their associate staff as members of their board, while others allow them to attend part or all of the meetings but do not allow them to vote. Still others do not include them on the board at all. Of the thriving associate staff members who participated in the first study (1996–97), about 75 percent attended church board meetings, and 50 percent of those were voting members. Whatever your policy and practices about board membership and voting privileges, consider at least doing the following:

- Provide a time at your board meetings when associate staff members can share a report about how their ministries are going, including the needs or challenges they face and good things that are happening. (If you have many associate staff members, this may have to be done on a rotating basis.)
- Where appropriate, make associate staff aware of the issues the board is dealing with and ask if they have any questions or insights to share.
- Take time to pray with associate staff for personal and ministry needs.

Doing these things helps build a good working relationship between associates and board, keeps them informed of issues that may have an impact on their ministry areas, provides them a chance to share their perspectives and be heard, and encourages unity in prayer together.

If you do have associate staff members attend board meetings when ministry policies and plans are being discussed, be sure to create an environment that encourages them to share what they really think about the items you are discussing. You will want to discuss this with your senior pastor, and not all will be equally comfortable with the idea, but there is value in having this kind of openness in board discussions. Sometimes associate staff members don't say what they think for fear that if it is contrary to their senior pastor's views, they will appear to be disloyal or divisive. From my perspective, loyalty is shown not by being a yes-man or yes-woman in the decision-making process but by supporting the decisions of the senior pastor and board once they are made. If an associate staff member has concerns about a decision being made by the board and does not make these concerns known, I would consider that disloyal. However, once a decision is made, the associate staff member must support the board in its decision and not complain about it to others.

Provide Opportunities for Growth and Renewal

Associate staff members appreciate serving in churches that provide them opportunities to continue to grow in ministry vision and skills. They value being exposed to new ideas and ways of doing ministry, being challenged to evaluate their ministries and to find ways to be more effective, and having time for their own spiritual renewal. As a church board, consider how you can invest in the ongoing growth and renewal of all staff members. Here are some things that associate staff members say they benefit from most.

Provide Opportunities for Continuing Education

Associate staff members want to keep learning and growing in ministry effectiveness. Having the time and money available to attend professional conferences, to take classes at a local seminary or university, to participate in ministry workshops, or even to pursue a degree in their ministry area makes possible these growth opportunities. Consider how your board could make continuing-education opportunities, formal or nonformal, available to all staff. These experiences help motivate them and renew their energies as well as provide them with new ideas and insights that can promote increased ministry effectiveness. Continuing education is an investment in your staff members and your congregation. Make sure you provide them with both the time and the money to make these benefits possible.

Support Associate Staff Members' Growing Vision for Ministry

Every associate staff member comes into a church with a vision of what his or her ministry can be. As time progresses, the person's understanding of the needs and resources of the congregation and community grows, and his or her ministry vision grows and changes as well. Your board can be of great help in this process. You can start by helping staff members understand the church's vision for ministry and how their own ministry area ties into the larger picture. Encourage associate staff to share their vision for ministry with you, and as you see them dreaming about a possible future, support them in exploring what steps need to be taken to get there. Your associate staff members don't want to do just ministry maintenance. They want to be used by God to help the church extend its outreach and improve its ministry effectiveness. Encourage them to keep pursuing this aim, and help them persevere as they work toward it.

Regularly Review and Update Associates' Job Descriptions

Associate staff members find that the demands of their jobs change over time, and new opportunities come for them to exercise their gifts and abilities in ways that were not part of the original job description. They appreciate having a job description that allows them to respond to changing ministry demands and grow on the job, and that leaves room for God to draw out new gifts for ministry. Don't expect the job descriptions of associate staff to remain static, but encourage regular times for evaluation and assessment. For example, a youth pastor may see the need for a new college ministry and want to add that to her responsibilities. Or the worship pastor may see the potential of starting a new music group for children. These times of job description revision can allow the ministry gifts of your staff to blossom on the job. Annual reviews of the position description and discussions about new ministry possibilities are a great place to start.

Encourage Personal and Staff Retreats

Spiritual growth and renewal are a must for those who serve on staff in your congregation. Your staff members face many stresses in ministry, and they can easily find themselves caring for the spiritual needs of others and not having adequate time available for their own spiritual nurture. Encourage staff to take time for both group and individual retreats for spiritual renewal. Help associates locate retreat sites and provide funding to make their time away possible. This is a critical investment that pays off in the ministries that flow out of their walk with God.

Also, consider holding an annual joint retreat of board and staff. The focus of this retreat should not be business or ministry issues but growth together in your walk with God. These experiences can unite you in your ministry vision and build bonds of fellowship that enhance your ability to minister together.

Respond to Associates' Personal Needs

Your associate staff members are employees of the church, but they are also your brothers and sisters in Christ and members of your fellowship. It is important to see them as people God has called you to care for, not just supervise. Your board can respond to the personal and family needs of the church's associate staff members in several ways, helping them thrive as they serve your congregation.

Provide Adequate Compensation and Benefits

Associate staff members who feel that they are thriving in their work report that their congregations pay them adequate salary and benefits to provide for themselves and their families. One reason that some associate staff members look for new ministry positions or leave church staff ministry altogether is a lack of adequate pay. Associate staff members have a basic need to provide for themselves and their families. As their families grow and financial demands increase, they sometimes find that their church salaries do not keep pace. How is your church doing in this area?

Churches often stretch their budgets to bring on new associate staff members, and they may be unsure what kind of compensation package is fair. They may also find themselves fighting the temptation to pay as little as they can to get or keep someone. If you take seriously your church's responsibility to provide for those who serve on church staff (1 Tim. 5:17), then give careful consideration to how you provide for their financial needs. Here are some guidelines that may help meet their needs.

Base salary. One standard for comparison that works well in many communities is to look at what public-school teachers with comparable education and experience earn. Remember, while the schoolteachers are on a nine- or ten-month contract, associate staff members will serve your congregation year-round.

Ministry expenses. If the associate staff member will use his or her own car for church business and purchase books and other materials for ministry use, develop a budget for compensation.

Health and life insurance. Be sure associate staff members have adequate health insurance to address their individual and family needs and life insurance to provide for them.

Retirement program. If your denomination or congregation has a retirement plan for your senior pastor, be sure to extend the same benefit to associate staff members. This benefit will encourage their longevity in ministry.

Vacation time and sabbaticals. Think through your policies on vacation time and extended breaks or sabbaticals for study and renewal. Vacation time should be long enough for personal renewal and the opportunity to see extended family. Sabbaticals for study could be part of a package that encourages longevity in ministry. Whatever you do, make it consistent with all your staff.

Continuing education. This topic was discussed above. Be sure that you are providing the opportunity for associate staff to participate in programs and events that will encourage them and enhance their ministry knowledge and skills.

Tax status. One way you can help associate staff members is to allow them to pursue licensing or ordination, if that is possible. There is no telling how long the U.S. government will continue to grant licensed and ordained church workers favorable tax status with regard to housing costs, but as long as there is benefit to your associate staff, give them the opportunity to pursue it if you can.

Allow Flexibility in the Work Schedule

Time demands on people in ministry tend to change with the calendar. When I was on staff, my busiest months were August through October and March through June. When I carried youth-ministry responsibilities, summers were busy as well. There were times during the year when I was out five to six nights a week, and many entire weekends were taken up with retreats or youth trips. When associate staff face busy evenings and weekends, they appreciate being able to take time off without guilt to make up for the extra time they are putting in. In addition, having flexibility to take time out of the office for their own children's school programs or to work at home so that they can care for a sick child or spouse is deeply appreciated. This flexibility reduces the stress they feel in meeting ministry and family needs and helps family members appreciate the church instead of resenting its demands on the staff member. If you have women associate staff with children at home or elderly family members to care for, this may be an especially important service you can offer them, given that many women still carry primary responsibility for family life.

Build a Personal Support Team for Associate Staff

Associate staff members are answerable to their ministry supervisor (generally the senior pastor) and to the committees and boards they report to and work with. While these people can be very supportive, associate staff members may be hesitant to share some struggles and concerns with them. Associate staff can benefit greatly from having a small group of people to meet with whose sole focus is to support them, listen to them, and pray for them. They need a place to be loved and cared for, knowing that whatever they say will remain confidential. If a group like this is to be formed, it should be developed by the staff member so that she is comfortable with its purpose and those who are a part of it. It may be that she has already addressed this need in other ways, such as meeting with a mentor outside the church or participating in a support group of peers from other churches. If not, consider if there is a way to address this within your congregation with mature lay leaders who can focus on care and support for the staff member. Some congregations have a personnel committee that is designed for these kinds of needs.

Respond to Critical Personal and Family Needs

There was a time when I faced a crisis in my family that affected my ability to keep up with the demands of my staff position. I was answerable to two boards, and I shared my problem with the chairs of both boards. Each chair called a special board meeting for me to explain my situation and say which tasks I felt I needed to back off from in my work for the time being. In each case, board members listened to me, affirmed me and my decisions, and prayed for me. In a follow-up, two lay leaders paid a visit to my home, told us how God had worked through their own family crises, and prayed with us. While the crisis we faced was difficult, the response of the church to our needs was a tremendous blessing to my family and me. The lay leaders let me know that they cared about me and my family and were willing to pray for me, weep with me, and rejoice with me. Care for your staff and make sure they know that the church will come alongside them in times of need.

Other Ways to Help Associate Staff Thrive

A few remaining items are important in supporting your associate staff.

Support Your Senior Pastor or Staff Supervisor

The church staff person who directly supervises the associate staff probably has the greatest influence on their longevity and satisfaction in ministry. This person has the challenge of both holding them accountable for their ministry efforts and supporting them in the process, while carrying out his own ministry responsibilities. It is not an easy task! This person will need your encouragement and support as he strives to do this well. Consider occasionally taking some time in your board meetings to focus on this person's work as a ministry supervisor—what's going well, what is a struggle, what help is needed. If appropriate, encourage him to attend a course or seminar on supervising associate staff or multiple-staff ministry issues. Look for ways to help the ministry supervisor gain the skills and receive the support needed for this important part of his work. (Chapter 10 offers suggestions for the supervisor of associate staff members.)

Encourage Commitment and Dependability among Lay Leaders

One of the greatest pleasures for associate staff is to work with lay volunteers who are committed to their ministry areas and dependable in carrying out their responsibilities. This assistance eliminates many of the headaches of ministry, freeing the staff member to equip and support these people in their ministries. Your board can help by finding ways to reinforce in the congregation the value of the church's ministries and the importance of people following through with their ministry commitments. You can pursue the development of a congregationwide gifts-assessment and ministry-recruitment process that helps people find ministry opportunities that use their gifts and match their priorities and availability. You can encourage ministry groups to have dedication ceremonies for their leaders; regular meetings for support, planning, and skill development; and times of celebration for ministry accomplishments. All these can help create a climate that encourages commitment and dependability in the volunteers that your associate staff will work with.

Ask How You Can Help

Finally, do not assume that you know what your associate staff people need to thrive in ministry. Take time to ask how they are doing and how their ministries are going. Listen as they share what God is doing and the challenges they face. Ask what you as individuals and as a board can do to help in their ministries. Just to be asked and listened to will mean a lot to them. Whatever they share in answer to your questions, listen carefully and see what steps you can take to support them as they serve your church.

Taking Inventory: Questions for Reflection and Discussion

Some of the questions that follow may be good for you to think about first and then to discuss with others on your board. Some you may want to talk over with the senior pastor, and others you may want to talk about with your congregation's associate staff members. Each church situation is unique, and these questions may trigger other issues that would be more helpful for you and your board to consider. Use these questions in ways that will be of the most help to you and your church staff.

Creating a Supportive Ministry Environment

1. How is the general *relational health* of your church? What problem areas need the attention of your church board?
2. When was the last time board members personally affirmed your associate staff for their ministry gifts and expressed your appreciation to them for the ways they serve your church?

3. Who on your staff tends to function more behind the scenes and may benefit from some special encouragement and appreciation?
4. Do the titles you use for your associate staff encourage the respect you would like members of your congregation to have for them?
5. If ordination or licensing is not possible for some of your associate staff, how else can you promote congregational support for them in their calling to serve the church?
6. Does the congregation see and hear from each of your associate staff often enough to know who they are and to appreciate their contributions to your congregation?
7. How can you encourage congregation members to express their support and appreciation for your associate staff members?
8. Are you providing the authority and financial resources your associate staff need to carry out their ministries well?
9. Do you as a board have enough times of fellowship with your church staff? Are you getting to know them as people, or do you just know what they do for the congregation?
10. Are you praying regularly *for* your associate staff members? Are you taking time to find out how you can pray best for them, and are you praying *with* them as well?

Providing Associate Staff the Opportunity to Lead

1. Have you clarified with associate staff members what their job responsibilities are and your expectations of them as staff members? Have you clarified what they can expect from the board?
2. How does the board tend to respond to new ideas for ministry changes from your associate staff members? Do your responses encourage or stifle their initiative and creativity? Are you turning them into ministry maintainers or allowing them to be ministry leaders?
3. In what ways are you willing to have associate staff members participate on this board?
   a. Do you want them occasionally to bring reports, share their needs, and have the board pray for them?

b. Do you want them present at all or most of your meetings and to be able to voice their opinions on issues the board addresses?

c. Do you want them to function as full members of the board, except in those areas where their own work is to be evaluated?

d. If they do attend portions or all of your meetings where decisions are being made, do you encourage them to share their views?

Providing Associate Staff Opportunities to Grow

1. Are you providing adequate time and financial support for your associate staff members to pursue continuing-education opportunities? Are you aware of what opportunities they would like to take advantage of if they were able to?

2. Do you encourage your associate staff to share ministry dreams and goals with the board? Do you support them in these pursuits?

3. Does the board regularly review the job descriptions of associate staff, providing the opportunity for revisions as ministry gifts, needs, and opportunities change?

4. Is the congregation providing opportunities and financial support for staff to have group and individual retreats for their own spiritual renewal?

5. When was the last time you had a retreat together with all your staff members, seeking to grow together in Christ? When could you do this again?

Responding to Associate Staff Personal Needs

1. How do the compensation and benefit packages for your associate staff compare with those of public-school teachers (with similar education and experience) in your community? If you think this does not seem to be an appropriate comparison, what standard do you want to use?

2. Have you done a cost-of-living analysis of what it takes to live in your community and provide for families the size of those of your associate staff members?

3. Are you providing adequate ministry expense reimbursement, health and life insurance, retirement plan, vacation time, and continuing-education opportunities for your associate staff?
4. Is there adequate flexibility of work schedule for staff members to allow them to meet personal and family needs and to balance periods of intense ministry involvement with time off for renewal?
5. Do associate staff members have people in the congregation who function as a support team for them? If not, would they like the board to help bring this about, or do they have adequate support in other ways?
6. Is the board attentive to the personal and family needs of staff? Do you have a relationship with them that helps you be aware of these needs, or are you pretty much unaware of their lives outside their work?

Other Items

1. In what ways are you supporting the senior pastor or other supervisor of associate staff in his or her responsibilities? In what ways could the board offer more support?
2. In what ways are you encouraging the members of the congregation to be faithful in their ministries? What else could you do?
3. Have you taken time to sit and listen to your associate staff members and to find out how they would like you to support them in their ministries? If not, when can you do this?

Appendix A

The "Thriving in Associate Staff Ministry" Studies

Study 1, Phase 1: Focus Group Research

From March 1996 to February 1997, twenty-one focus groups were conducted in two types of settings. Some were held in the greater Los Angeles area with local long-term associate staff members. Others were held across the United States and Canada in various cities and at national professional gatherings of associate staff.

Table 1. Types and Locations of Focus Groups

Ministry Group	Number	Description
Children's ministry staff	3	1 at Church Min. Conf., Hume Lake, CA, 5/96 2 at Children's Pastors Conf., San Diego, CA, 2/97
Youth ministry staff	3	1 in Los Angeles, CA, 5/96 2 at Youth Specialties Conf., Irvine, CA, 11/96
General Christian ed. staff	3	1 at Church Min. Conf., Hume Lake, CA, 5/96 2 at Christian Educators' Conf., Dallas, TX, 1/97
Music and worship staff	3	1 in Los Angeles, CA, 6/96 2 at MusiCalifornia Conf., San Diego, CA, 4/96
Women associate staff	3	1 in Los Angeles, CA, 5/96 1 at Women's Min. Conf., Pasadena, CA, 3/96 1 at Church Min. Conf., Hume Lake, CA, 5/96
Black church staff	2	1 in Los Angeles, CA, 2/97 1 in Dallas, TX, 1/97
Canadian church staff	2	1 in Toronto, Ontario, Canada, 6/96 1 in Calgary, Alberta, Canada, 2/97
Associate pastors	1	1 in Dallas, TX, 1/97
Part-time associate staff	1	1 at Church Min. Conf., Hume Lake, CA, 5/96

These focus groups allowed the participants to identify and describe what was helping them thrive in ministry, not just survive. Transcripts were made of focus-group discussions. These were reviewed; the range of issues related to thriving in associate staff ministry was noted. Explanatory comments were analyzed to discern why these issues were important and what contributed to their influence and development. Comparisons were made between groups with similar ministry responsibilities and between different types of groups. The common issues were overwhelming, with few items applicable to only one type of associate staff position. Overall, seventy-three items were repeated by participants in multiple focus groups, eighteen of which related specifically to the supervising pastor. These items were included in the survey developed for Phase 2 of the study.

Study 1, Phase 2: Survey of Long-Term Associate Staff

A survey instrument was put together and sent to long-term (seven years' ministry experience or more) associate staff members in fourteen cooperating denominations across the United States and Canada. The denominations that participated in the survey portion of this study included the following (shown with number of people included and response rates).

Table 2. Denominations Participating in the Survey

Denominations	Number	Responses	Response Rate
US Denominations:			
American Baptist	58	23	40%
Assemblies of God	60	34	57%
Black church staff	71	15	21%
(African Methodist, Episcopal,			
Southern Baptist, American Baptist)			
Christian & Missionary Alliance	56	39	70%
Conservative Baptist	63	35	56%
Evangelical Covenant	28	20	71%
Missouri Synod Lutheran	61	24	39%
Presbyterian (USA)	58	38	66%
Southern Baptist	42	23	55%
United Methodist	65	36	55%
Previous focus group participants	102	67	66%

Denominations	Number	Responses	Response Rate
Canadian Denominations:			
Christian & Missionary Alliance	30	26	87%
Mennonite Brethren	10	7	70%
Pentecostal Assemblies	29	23	79%
United Church of Canada	29	23	79%
Previous focus group participants	13	12	92%
Totals	**775**	**445**	**57%**

The response rates varied greatly from one denomination to another. This discrepancy was due partly to the fact that some denominations had a more difficult time than others in keeping current records on those who serve in associate staff capacities in local churches. Of the 445 responses, 27 were eliminated because the respondent was not thriving in ministry, and four were removed because they had less than the minimum seven years of associate ministry experience. The final result was 414 usable surveys.

Table 3. Summary of Information about the Survey Participants (n=414)

Gender	Male: 72%	Female: 28%	
Age	Mean: 47 years	Range: 27–81 years	
Ethnicity	Caucasian: 91%	Black: 5%	Other: 4%
Marital status	Single: 10%	Married: 90%	
Ordination status	Ordained: 66%	Licensed: 20%	Neither: 14%
Member of a professional association	Yes: 53%	No: 47%	
Highest degree earned	High School: 5%	BA/BS: 31%	
	MA/MDiv: 51%	Doctorate: 7%	Other: 4%
Majors	Ministry: 59%	Education (not CE): 23%	
	Business: 6%	Other: 25%	
Years associate staff	Mean: 14	Range: 7–51	
No. of churches served	Mean: 2.7	Range: 1–20	
Years in current church	Mean: 9	Range: 1–49	
Full-time vs. part-time	Full-time: 84%	Part-time: 16%	
Supervisor	Sr. pastor: 82%	Other: 18%	
Areas of ministry	Children: 29%	Youth: 27%	Adults: 31%
	Families: 24%	Music: 24%	All CE: 25%
	Assoc. Pastor: 36%	Women's Min.: 9%	Other: 44%
Country	USA: 79%	Canada: 21%	
Number on staff	Mean: 7	Range: 1–40	
Attend church board	Yes: 75%	No: 25%	

Study 2, Phase 1: Survey of Seminary Alumni (Associate Staff Members)

In spring 2012, we developed a survey based on the one used in the first study. We identified more than four hundred alumni from our seminary, Talbot School of Theology, with the help of Talbot Support Ministries (TSM). As a nondenominational seminary we have alumni serving in many different denominations. They are mostly serving churches on the West Coast of the United States, but there are alumni across the United States and in other countries as well. The survey was done electronically, using SurveyMonkey (www.surveymonkey .com). A series of three e-mails were sent to all the alumni identified. The first e-mail introduced the survey and invited their participation. Approximately one week later, a second e-mail was sent, reminding them of the value of the study and again encouraging their participation. Finally, about one week after the second e-mail, we sent one more, thanking those who had already participated in the study and urging others to respond before the survey time closed.

We received 188 usable survey responses from this group. We did not know ahead of time how many of these alumni had associate staff experience, so we were not sure what percentage would be able to respond to the survey. The data were analyzed and compared with the survey responses from the first study. In most cases the ratings for the level of influence of each item in the respondent's sense of thriving in ministry was similar to those in the 1996–97 study, and the percentage of people who identified the items as having an impact on their ability to thrive in ministry was similar or higher. The results of the second study confirmed that the things identified in the first study were still important. No new items emerged as having a strong influence on people's thriving in associate staff ministry. Some increases in percentage indicated that the things that help people thrive are widely influential, applicable to a high percentage of those who serve in these roles.

Study 2, Phase 2: Focus Group Research

Following the survey in spring 2012, we recruited about twenty Talbot alumni, both women and men, who were long-term associate staff members and thriving in their work to participate in focus group interviews with us. We met over lunches and spent 90 to 120 minutes discussing issues that stood out from the survey responses. The goal was to gain some explanations for the patterns we were seeing in the survey data, both in the ratings of "thriving items" and in the responses to the open-ended questions regarding advice to supervising pastors and to future associate staff members. Participants' perspectives and examples put more flesh on the issues we saw from the survey data and helped us better understand why certain things were so influential for thriving in associate staff roles. The input from these veteran associate staff members was invaluable in thinking through how to frame the presentations of the chapters and how certain things that had been identified as influential were related to each other. We deeply appreciate the time these veterans freely gave us and their willingness to be open about their experiences in ministry.

Survey Results: Comparison of 1996–97 and 2012 Studies

Study 1 survey participants: n=414 (Survey response rate = 57%)
Study 2 survey participants: n=182 (Survey response rate = 33%)

Interpretation of the numerical scores:

0	1	2	3	4	5
No influence	Slightly influential	Moderately influential	Very influential		

Factors are listed in order below based on their mean score in the 2012 study, from high to low. The numbers in the first column correspond to the question numbers in the survey.

Possible Thriving Factors				
		1996–97 Adjusted		**2012 Adjusted**	
		Mean	**%**	**Mean**	**%**
23.	A spouse who supports me in my ministry	4.6	87	4.7	92
43.	In my work, I seek God first, and strive to be open to his work in my life and through my life.	4.3	93	4.5	100
4.	A sense of fulfillment that comes from using my gifts/abilities in this way	4.4	99	4.4	100
16.	I see positive results of my ministry in the lives of those I minister to (lay leaders, participants)	4.3	97	4.3	100

		1996–97 Adjusted		2012 Adjusted	
		Mean	**%**	**Mean**	**%**
46.	I am committed to longevity in ministry and strive hard to persevere during difficult times	4.4	93	4.3	98
53.	I have developed a good awareness of my gifts/ abilities and this type of ministry is where I fit best	4.3	90	4.3	99
17.	A supportive work relationship with my senior pastor or supervisor	4.3	91	4.3	95
2.	A strong burden, passion, or vision for this kind/type of ministry	4.3	91	4.2	99
5.	The church is very supportive of my area of ministry (e.g., sense of importance, resources)	4.2	95	4.2	99
32.	I am a self-starter in my work and do not need much supervision	4.2	93	4.2	99
1.	A clear sense of calling from God to serve in an associate staff ministry role	4.4	92	4.2	97
8.	The church lay leadership support & believe in me	4.3	97	4.2	99
3.	Seeing my kind/type of ministry as "real ministry," not just a stepping stone to something else	4.6	98	4.2	97
44.	I experience great intimacy with God in worship	4.0	81	4.1	99
50.	I strive to keep my focus on the people I serve, not so much on the programs I run	4.1	89	4.1	99
15.	The church I serve is healthy and growing	4.1	88	4.1	97
18.	Good working relationships with the other associate staff in my church	4.0	86	4.1	96
33.	I strive to remain open to change, learn, grow	4.2	95	4.0	99
42.	I invest time regularly in studying the Bible for my own spiritual growth, not just for my ministry	3.9	82	4.0	99
9.	Flexibility to my work schedule allows me to care for my personal and/or family needs	4.0	91	4.0	98
47.	I have developed a spirit of contentment in my ministry	4.0	84	4.0	97
52.	I have a long-term ministry vision	4.1	79	4.0	96
10.	The lay staff I work with are committed/dependable	4.0	91	3.9	99
54.	Others have affirmed my gifts for ministry	4.4	96	3.9	100
14.	My job allows me to have input, and to exercise some leadership, in the broader church ministry	4.0	91	3.9	98
29.	I have been able to maintain a balance in my work and personal life	3.7	82	3.9	99
34.	I have a clear philosophy of ministry that guides and unifies my efforts in ministry	4.1	89	3.9	98
40.	Regular times for personal prayer	4.0	85	3.8	100
25.	Friendships with members of the congregation	3.9	93	3.8	99
51.	I am involved in mentoring others in ministry	4.1	74	3.8	95
22.	A mentor who I can turn to for counsel, or who serves as a model for me	3.7	51	3.8	90
7.	The church is open to new ideas, new ways of doing ministry (e.g., room for creativity)	4.0	93	3.7	96

		1996–97 Adjusted		2012 Adjusted	
		Mean	**%**	**Mean**	**%**
21.	Close supportive relationships with selected lay leaders or other members of the congregation	4.0	84	3.7	98
38.	I have learned how to handle tough times, to deal with discouragement, criticism, and difficult people	3.8	91	3.7	99
49.	I am committed to the success of my senior pastor, and I seek to find ways to support him	4.1	90	3.7	97
45.	Besides personal prayer and Bible study, and corporate worship, I have other spiritual disciplines that are an important part of my walk with God	3.9	61	3.6	95
12.	My job description is dynamic, with room for variety and change over time (new responsibilities)	3.9	83	3.6	92
6.	The church provides me with adequate pay and benefits to provide for myself/my family	3.7	90	3.6	90
13.	My job is fairly focused, allowing me to concentrate on one area of ministry that I love	3.7	59	3.6	87
55.	When I have interviewed at churches, I am very careful and thorough in checking out the pastor, the church, and the job before committing	4.1	52	3.6	75
11.	The church provides me with opportunities to pursue continuing education	3.5	84	3.5	84
24.	Family members (non-spouse) who support me	4.0	74	3.4	93
27.	I receive words or notes of appreciation and encouragement from those I minister with	4.0	74	3.4	95
31.	I focus my efforts on doing a few things well, and am able to say no to other requests	3.3	56	3.4	95
48.	I delegate a lot of ministry responsibilities to others, focusing my efforts in a few areas	3.5	59	3.4	95
20.	A prayer partner, or partners, who support me	3.9	58	3.4	93
28.	I receive words or notes of appreciation and encouragement from my senior pastor/supervisor	3.6	74	3.4	90
39.	As a staff, we enjoy socializing together	3.4	71	3.3	89
41.	I sometimes take extended times away in prayer, like a retreat or partial-day retreat	3.4	48	3.3	83
26.	Friendships with people outside my church	3.3	76	3.2	93
19.	Regular participation in an accountability or support group of peers in ministry	3.6	58	3.1	84
36.	I attend professional conferences, conventions, or other educational events for continuing growth and networking with others in my area of ministry	3.7	92	3.0	90
35.	I volunteer for ministry outside of my church (e.g., community, professional, denominational)	3.2	76	2.8	71
37.	I belong to a professional organization that focuses on my area of ministry	3.4	47	2.8	61
30.	The church staff having regular retreats together	3.3	47	2.6	71

Supervisor Issues

Possible Experiences with Supervisor	1996–97 Adjusted Mean	%	2012 Adjusted Mean	%
6. Demonstrate trust in me, his/her belief in my ministry abilities	4.4	92	4.4	99
8. Let me do my work without "looking over my shoulder" all the time	4.5	93	4.3	98
3. Treat me as a partner in ministry, part of the ministerial team, not just an assistant	4.5	89	4.2	98
7. Demonstrate loyalty to me as a ministry colleague	4.3	86	4.1	96
12. Not be threatened by my success in ministry	4.1	84	4.1	92
11. Demonstrate care about me, and love for me as a person, not just for what I do	4.0	82	4.0	95
2. Stand by me when I receive criticism	4.3	86	4.0	93
13. Maintain an "open door" policy, being available when I need to discuss something with him/her	4.3	89	3.9	97
15. Exhibit stability in his or her own ministry	4.2	83	3.9	94
4. Communicate his/her appreciation for my ministry efforts	4.0	85	3.8	98
16. Encourage my own spiritual growth and well-being	3.9	73	3.8	95
14. Demonstrate genuine interest in my area(s) of ministry	4.0	79	3.8	94
9. Communicate his ministry vision and philosophy for the church, and help me understand how what I do contributes to it	3.9	74	3.8	94
5. Encourage me to keep learning and growing personally and professionally	3.9	80	3.7	95
1. Hold regular (weekly or so) staff meetings	4.0	87	3.7	93
10. Encourage and affirm me when I am discouraged	3.9	73	3.7	91

Appendix B

Professional Organizations and Further Reading for Associate Staff

One key to thriving in associate staff ministry is developing supportive relationships with others familiar with the demands of your ministry responsibilities. Across North America, a large number of organizations sponsor conventions, conferences, and seminars where you can connect with others involved in your ministry area. Several groups maintain websites with information about training events, helpful resources, and chat rooms where you can talk with other associate staff members. Many cities and states have local organizations for associate staff based on common ministry responsibilities (for example, youth pastors, children's ministers, music ministers). Here are some suggestions for finding organizations that may be of help to you.

Denominational Groups

Be sure to make contact with your denominational leaders to see what networking groups and support organizations are active within your denomination for people involved in your kind of ministry. You may be surprised to learn that a group already exists, or you may discover others who desire to begin such a group. You could be a catalyst to help organize a group.

Community and Regional Groups

Many communities have ministerial fellowship groups. Some also have groups for those who focus their ministry efforts in a particular area, such as children's ministry, youth ministry, or worship. Check with church staff members in your area to see if they know of any groups that could be of benefit to you. If not, you may find a few people who would like to get together once a month for fellowship, troubleshooting, sharing of resource ideas, prayer, and maybe even some common ministry efforts. Again, you may be a catalyst to a group's formation.

National Organizations

There are a number of ways to locate national groups focused in your ministry area.

- Ask others you know who have the same ministry focus you do, especially those who have more years of experience.
- Check magazines or journals devoted to your ministry area. If you are not familiar with any, talk with others in your ministry area. A number of journals today address the needs of different ministry specialties.
- Search the Internet for websites devoted to your ministry area or to networking with people in your ministry area.

Starting Your Own Group

If there are no good options available for you to connect with others involved in your type of associate staff ministry, consider starting a small group to meet a few times a year to provide encouragement and support to one another. Others in your community or region may also value a regular gathering over a meal to share ideas, consider ways to be of support to each other, and possibly even work together on some common ministry efforts. Start by trying to identify one or two other associate staff members you can invite to join you for a meal or an evening to discuss the potential benefits of meeting together on a regular basis. Start small, and if you find it beneficial, reach out to others in your area who could benefit from this kind of group. If all else fails, you can connect with others you know via Skype or other similar methods, such as Google Hangout. While it may not be as good as actually being together, it may be the only way for you to develop the network you need for mutual support.

Further Reading for Associate Staff Members

While not a lot of books have been written for associate staff members, we have located some that you may want to consider reading. Some are older works but still worth reviewing. These may be a good resource to use when meeting together with fellow associate staff members, providing you with some ideas to reflect on and discuss together. Enjoy!

Bonem, Mike, and Roger Patterson. *Leading from the Second Chair: Serving Your Church, Fulfilling Your Role, and Realizing Your Dreams.* San Francisco: Jossey-Bass, 2005.

Burns, Bob, Tasha Chapman, and Donald C. Guthrie. *Resilient Ministry: What Pastors Told Us about Surviving and Thriving.* Downers Grove, IL: IVP Books, 2013.

Goode, Bernard P. *The Calling and Biblical Role of the Associate Minister.* Henrico, VA: Kingdom Publishing Group, 2010.

Hawkins, Martin E., and Kelli Sallman. *The Associate Pastor: Second Chair, Not Second Best.* Nashville: Broadman & Holman, 2005.

Hornsby, Billy. *Success for the Second in Command: Leading from the Second Chair.* Lake Mary, FL: Creation House, 2005.

Hopewell, David, Sr. *Keys to Becoming an Effective Associate Minister and Church Leader.* Lithonia, GA: Orman Press, 2004.

Nuechterlein, Anne Marie. *Improving Your Multiple Staff Ministry: How to Work Together More Effectively.* Minneapolis: Augsburg Fortress, 1989.

Nuechterlein, Anne Marie, and Celia Allison Hahn. *The Male-Female Church Staff: Celebrating the Gifts: Confronting the Challenges.* Herndon, VA: Alban Institute, 1990.

Oswald, Roy M. *Clergy Self-Care: Finding a Balance for Effective Ministry.* Herndon, VA: Alban Institute, 1991.

———. *How to Build a Support System for Your Ministry.* Herndon, VA: Alban Institute, 1991.

Patterson, Roger. *The Theology of the Second Chair: A Theological Foundation for the Subordinate Leader of the Local Church.* Raleigh, NC: Lulu.com, 2010.

Radcliffe, Robert J. *Effective Ministry as an Associate Pastor: Making Beautiful Music as a Ministry Team.* Grand Rapids: Kregel, 1998.

Sheets, Dutch, and Chris Jackson. *Second in Command: Strengthening Leaders Who Serve Leaders.* Shippensburg, PA: Destiny Image, 2005.

Westing, Harold J. *Multiple Church Staff Handbook.* Rev. ed. Grand Rapids: Kregel, 1998.

Williams, Benny L. *Called, Trained, and Ordained: The Work of the Associate Minister in the Local Church.* Bloomington, IN: Xlibris, 2009.

Notes

Introduction to the Second Edition: A Model for Thriving in Associate Staff Ministry

1. Paul H. Veith, *The Church and Christian Education* (St. Louis: Bethany Press, 1947), 200.

Chapter 1: Finding Satisfaction in Following God's Call

1. Ben Patterson, "Is Ministry a Career?" *Leadership*, Summer 1990, 54.

2. H. Richard Niebuhr, Daniel Day Williams, and James M. Gustafson, *The Purpose of the Church and Its Ministry: Reflections on the Aims of Theological Education.* (New York: Harper & Row, 1956), 64.

3. Ibid.

4. Ibid.

5. John Newton, quoted in "How Do I Know I'm Called?" *Leadership*, Summer 1990, 55–56. Newton's response was originally published in 1787.

6. Niebuhr, Williams, and Gustafson, *Purpose of the Church*, 64.

Chapter 2: Sustaining Spiritual Vitality in Ministry

1. Eugene Peterson, *Under the Unpredictable Plant: An Exploration in Vocational Holiness* (Grand Rapids: Eerdmans, 1992), 4.

2. Peterson, *Under the Unpredictable Plant*, 1–3. Reprinted by permission of the publisher, all rights reserved.

Chapter 4: Strengthening the Home Front

1. These recommendations for coping with stress are adapted from Walter H. Gmelch, *Coping with Faculty Stress* (Thousand Oaks, CA: Sage Publications, 1993), and from Gwen S. Faulkner and Terry D. Anderson, *Stress Indicator and Health Planner* (Sumas, WA: Consulting Resources Group, 1990).

Chapter 7: Attitudes and Commitments That Support Thriving

1. Eugene Peterson, *Under the Unpredictable Plant: An Exploration in Vocational Holiness* (Grand Rapids: Eerdmans, 1992).

Chapter 9: When You're Not Thriving

1. D. J. Levinson, *The Seasons of a Man's Life* (New York: Alfred A. Knopf, 1978), 97.
2. Ibid., 98.
3. Michael J. Anthony and Mick Boersma, *Moving On–Moving Forward: A Guide for Pastors in Transition* (Grand Rapids: Zondervan, 2007), 85–99.

Chapter 10: The Valued Ministry Supervisor

1. Stephen R. Covey, *The 7 Habits of Highly Effective People* (New York: Simon & Schuster, 1989), 287.

CPSIA information can be obtained at www.ICGtesting.com
Printed in the USA
BVOW07s1156180714

359470BV00002B/2/P